Diaspora 2

Re-Thinking *The Godfather* 50 Years Later

Edited by
Anthony Julian Tamburri

CASA LAGO PRESS
NEW FAIRFIELD, CT

Diaspora
Volume 2

As "diaspora" is the dispersion or spread of people from their original homeland, this book series takes its name in the intellectual spirit of willful dispersion of subject matter and thought. It is dedicated to publishing those studies that in various and sundry ways either speak to or offer new methods of analysis of the Italian diaspora.

The publication of this book has bene made possible through a generous grant from an anonymous donor who wishes not to be identified but urges others to donate to historical and cultural studies.

COVER PHOTO: Tina Modotti, "Hands of the Puppeteer," 1929
Minneapolis Institute of Art

COVER DESIGN: Nicholas Grosso

ISBN 978-1-955995-06-1
Library of Congress Control Number: Available upon request

CASA LAGO PRESS
New Fairfield, CT

TABLE OF CONTENTS

PREFACE

Francis Ford Coppola's *The Godfather* has been heralded as one of the best films ever. On the other hand, it has also been condemned for it seeming glorification of organized crime and, more specifically, the Mafia. Indeed, such criticism supposedly moved the then dubious Italian American Civil Rights League to force Coppola not to include the term "mafia," according to many accounts over the years, the latest by Mark Seal in his *Leave the Gun, Take the Cannoli* (2021). Nonetheless, the film, as well, has been excoriated for having been the inspiration for hundreds of subsequent films of Italians and organized crime.[1]

The late Dr. Anne Paolucci, Professor of English at St. John's University and once Chair of the Board of Trustees of The City University of New York, saw such criticism by Italian Americans as misplaced defensiveness of anti-Italian discrimination. She stated the following in one of her last essays: "'discrimination' carries little weight when leveled against the producers of such profitable television series as *The Sopranos* (with a large audience) or such films as *The Godfather* — *a genial account*, among other things, of the power assumed by a few strong men to protect themselves and their community in the early days, when Italians had to deal with a hostile environment and had to turn to their own, for justice.... [A]re we pressing the wrong buttons? Do we really expect Hollywood to apologize for *The Godfather*? Why should it? The film has

---

[1] Both Bill Dal Cerro and Ben Lawton deal with this issue from two slightly different perspectives.

become a classic and with good reason: *it's one of the best ever made, with a superb cast; a realistic account of the hostility between the Irish and the Italians, in the early days*; a drama of power as it takes on the law, and of gradual changes that came about within the 'families' at that time. In the end, of course, all arguments disappear: *it's only fiction ... but also a piece of history*" (16-17; my emphasis).

This collection of essays looks at all aspects of Coppola's "classic," as Paolucci called it. The individual studies examine a series of issues that are both thematic and structural. How did the film speak to us in 1972, and how does it speak to us now? What narrative devices did Coppola adopt to bring forth his communiqué? Can we decipher what his communiqué was? In viewing the film from a more theoretical perspective, what can the spectator take away from the film?

It is the notion of spectatorship, and whether we can develop other characteristics to this individual, that convinced me to take a second look at an essay I had originally published in 2011. As I examined other films and written texts in the subsequent baker's dozen years, I realized that through theories and methodologies such as semiotics, hermeneutics, reader-response reception, and affect theory, we can approach the cinematic text in a manner analogous — not identically — to how we approach the written text.

Much has been written in the past few years on Francis Ford Coppola's *The Godfather* series. Here, I cite one of the more recent publications, Mark Seal's *Leave the Gun, Take the Cannoli*, which opens a new window to the production of Coppola's series. Most other publications we have seen lately — essays and books — are either quite personal in manner, which does not interest us here, or a re-packaging of previous notions through more sophisticated vocabulary of seemingly new methodologies.[2]

Conversely, the contributors to this volume all draw to some degree from any of the above-mentioned theories and methodologies, and their essays bring forth, each one in its own right, new ways of viewing Francis Ford Coppola's *The Godfather* series. In a similar manner, I had subsequently returned to texts such as Pietro di Donato's *Christ in Concrete* (Tamburri 2020) and Martin Scorsese's *Mean Streets* (Tamburri 2017) with the goal of re-examining both the functionality — read, also, the user's intentionality — of code-switching and that of the related comparison between the "uninformed" and the "informed Italian/American reader and/or spectator."[3]

WORKS CITED

Dal Cerro, William. 1997. "Hollywood versus Italians: Them–400, Us–50." *The Italic Way* 27: 10-11, 30-32.

Lawton, Ben. 2002. "Mafia and the Movies: Why Is Italian American Synonymous with Organized Crime?" 69-95. Anna Camaiti Hostert and Anthony Julian Tamburri, eds. *Screening Ethnicity. Cinematographic Representations of Italian Americans in the United States*. Boca Raton: Bordighera Press.

---

[2] Given that this is a preface to a collection of new studies and not a review essay, I shall resort to the Italian saying, "si dice il peccato ma non il peccatore" (one mentions the sin but not the sinner).

[3] All images in this book were personally extracted from the film and are used here in accordance with the specifications of § 107 in *Copyright Law of the United States* (2022): "[F]air use of a copyrighted work [...] for purposes such as criticism, comment, news reporting, teaching..., scholarship, or research, is not an infringement of copyright."

Paolucci, Anne. 2007. "Preserving the Future through the Past (A Personal Assessment)." In *Italian American Perspectives*. New York: Griffon House.

Seal, Mark. 2021. *Leave the Gun, Take the Cannoli: The Epic Story of the Making of* The Godfather. New York: Gallery Books.

Tamburri, Anthony Julian. 2020. "La diacriticità e lo scrittore italiano/americano: Il trattino come confine linguistico e l'"intelligibilità reciproca" in *Christ in Concrete* (1939) di Pietro di Donato," *Campi immaginabili* 62-63. 363-389.

Tamburri, Anthony Julian. 2017. "Il sistema di segni del cinema italiano/americano: *code-switching* e la significabilità di *Mean Streets* di Martin Scorsese," *Ácoma* (Fall-Winter): 108-121.

Tamburri, Anthony Julian. 2011. "Michael Corleone's Tie: Francis Ford Coppola's *The Godfather*" in *Mafia Movies. A Reader*. Dana Renga, ed. Toronto: U Toronto P. 94-101. Slightly modified as "Michael Corleone's Tie: Francis Ford Coppola's *The Godfather* and the Rhetoric of Antinomy," it reappeared in my *Re-viewing Italian Americana: Generalities and Specificities on Cinema*. New York: Bordighera Press, 2011. 80-91.

No Girls Allowed
Homosociality and the Man Caves of Identity

DONNA M. CHIRICO

It may seem out of place for a developmental psychologist to be commenting upon film, but, of course, it is not the form, *per se*, that has attracted the attention of the social sciences. Cinema and novels provide characterizations of the human experience unmatched by any course textbook. In fact, when teaching the course on Adolescent and Adult development, I do not assign a textbook, they all say the same thing — Freud this, Piaget that — but instead ask students to choose from and read a selection of novels that follow each phase of the lifespan. When I teach the course, the "Italian American Experience in the United States," I do so from the perspective of identity development and self-identity to consider the intersections of ethnicity, gender, sexuality, race, and other aspects of the self to illustrate how these come together to establish a sense of overall psychological identity. In discussing the place and influence of the mafia in the United States and elsewhere, it is presented as part of identity development for those who are attracted to such enterprises and such entertainments. This is done through film and literature.

Regarding the emphasis on Italian American ethnicity and identity in the genre of gangster movies, one must trace the path from 1930s to the present. Just as identity develops through time, so does the way film portrays individual characters. In my course, I begin with clips from

The Public Enemy (1931) and *Scarface* (1932) to illustrate how the representation of the gangster moves from completely not Italian or Italian American — James Cagney as Tom Powers — to Italian or Italian American played by actors with no Italian heritage — Paul Muni as Tony Camonte — to eventually those films where Italian Americans, for the most part, play themselves including Al Pacino in the remake of *Scarface* but with now the character's name changed to the easier to pronounce Tony Montana instead of Camonte.

The reality is that in the United States there were well-established and well-organized crime syndicates before the arrival of Italian immigrants. As immigrant groups arrived, these criminal organizations were run by Irish, Poles, Russians, and Jews. In the present, new immigrant groups from Central America and Asia have established themselves as the crime bosses. Students of varying ethnicity in my course relate to this because they know how the mafias of their cultures operate and the teachery involved. Interestingly, they have said how proud they feel when there is a mafia movie or series about their group such as the Netflix series about Pablo Escobar, because it indicates the status of their ethnic group. Note too, the current 10 Most Wanted Fugitives list of the FBI is dominated by Latinx names, plus it includes a man from India and a woman from Bulgaria. Since the FBI began publishing the list in 1950, there have been 26 Italian or Italian Americans out of approximately 526 fugitives on the list, that is less than 5% and most were in the early decades of the process (Federal Bureau of Investigation 2023).

George De Stefano, documents how the image of the gangster became Italian American, and how the character of those participating in organized crime became more sinister, especially after World War II. He states, "Italian gangsters were less visible in popular culture during the 1940s, when Nazis and other monsters, usually supernatural became Hollywood's designated bad guys. But they reemerged in the 1950s and 60s, in popular television series such as *The Untouchables* and movies like Capone. De Stefano continues about the significance of the fictional characters that, "...were representations of real-life criminal conspirators who posed a grave threat to the nation" (2007, 344).

Separate from its value as a pedagogical tool, research tells us that *The Godfather* has contributed to how personal identity develops; hence, the aim in this paper is to illustrate how the film has contributed to the development of masculine identity in the Italian American community and beyond. That the film has had a remarkable influence is clear, it is a part of broader culture in many ways, but that *The Godfather* and other films of this genre do contribute to the development of individual personality and can transform the path of psychological development is less obvious and requires research evidence.

It must be stated too that personal interaction with any social media varies from person to person. In the early 1960s when the presence of a television in the home became ubiquitous and was seen as the bogeyman of the age, psychologists were eager to show how the new medium would destroy children's social development and govern their behavior. In his initial and highly flawed Bobo Doll studies, Albert Bandura together with Dorothea and Sheila Ross (1961) claimed that seeing adults model aggressive behavior made young children more aggressive.

It is now understood that the influence, positive or negative, and outcomes of modeling behavior depends on numerous other, sometimes confounding, variables (Bar On 2001). Changes in technology and media are regularly studied and evaluated across disciplines. The American Academy of Pediatrics has published meta-analyses of such work with a focus on the effects of media violence (2001). A central issue when violence takes hold is an inability to distinguish reality from fantasy. This cognitive capacity is underdeveloped in children under the age of eight because the frontal lobe is not well developed at this point (Rosch and Mostofsky 2019). This failure of separating the real from the imagined is studied today as we see older "children" act as if this function is not developed or does not exist. The results are typically self-harm or harming others, usually without fully comprehending the action or its consequences. The media is quick to cite "mental illness" when the criminal is underage, yet the lack or inhibition of cognitive development can lead to a failure in hindering the self-regulating capacity of the conscience. The ability to limit negative behaviors through the guilt and mental anguish aroused in the psyche are diminished or lost.

There are two threads that guide this exploration of how *The Godfather* can play a role in identity development. One is the influence on the development of a masculine identity and the other is how this identity is shaped by being with other men, in this case within a specific subgroup — Italian American men.

4

This topic of masculine identity and the influences upon its development have been broached in different ways by different disciplines. The field of masculinity studies looks at how myriad variables, alone or in combination, direct the course of psychological development. The influence of the body and body image, societal norms, and expectations, and more explicitly, community and ethnic expectations all contribute to how a boy decides to move into manhood.

I am exclusively speaking about individuals who identify as male, hence, the use of the gendered terminology. Identity research on those who are trans or non-binary is a growing field that has yet to adequately address race, and even less explored is ethnicity.

From this work on the interactions of male identity development with other aspects of development, much has been learned about the patterns of positive and negative identity formation. For example, there is ample research about the timing of certain aspects of physical development; puberty has been widely studied with an awareness that very early or very later physical development can be detrimental. This has been particularly the case for late maturing boys, who may be directly bullied by others and who see media images of the idealized 13- or 14-year-old male body. The resulting problems that emerge such as depression and lowered self-esteem become adult traits difficult to overcome. Research about the physical aspects of identity has predominantly studied girls because the rates of faulty behaviors tend to be higher, but there is evidence that negative behavior in boys tends to be more severe (Rudolf et al. 2014).

The Godfather sends both positive and negative messages about ways of being in the world. The violence shown in this film, or any other media rarely has the wide-spread effect people fear unless there are other factors involved. Watching violence alone does not lead to committing acts of violence in the majority of people. This is a simplistic idea that study upon study has debunked. Violence is not the only negative behavior seen in *The Godfather*, nor perhaps the most insidious. The place and treatment of women reinforces patriarchic attitudes embedded in the culture of the film's day and persist into the present despite an awareness of the inherent misogyny. Throughout the film, women are denigrated or infantilized or simply disregarded. In the closing scene of the film the doors to the inner sanctum are closed to Kay both literally and figuratively and, of course, the histrionics and tantrums of Connie.

Escaping assigned societal roles is a difficult process requiring a cognitive reassessment of the self; escaping assigned ethnic roles is an even greater challenge because of the pressures from the family and the surrounding ethnic community on the avenues of individual choice. Guilt, shame, and powerlessness or what is called learned helplessness prevent action on the part of the individual to make substantive change. The person believes there is no escape. At the start of *The Godfather*, Michael states that he is not like his family and has no interest in the family business, but in what seems like the inevitable, through circumstances seemingly out of his control, he takes on the role he vilified. The actuality that Michael makes a choice is blurred.

Further, the persistent emphasis on abnormal or aberrant behavior in media detracts from the work of those researchers who are interested in the behaviors, learned and inherent, that are affirming. These are those aspects that help to build a strong sense of self helping the individual find purpose in life and flourish. Maslow's concept of self-actualization and the area of Positive Psychology he helped to form, looks at the human condition with an optimistic eye quite different from Freud and the neo-Freudians. Positive Psychology has been associated in the last decade with the likes of Martin Seligman, who books have popularized the idea by emphasizing happiness, well-being, and quality of life. Unfortunately, this wider popularization has been commodified so that self-care is assumed to be a nice, warm bubble bath and glass of wine rather than the processes of self-reflection and evaluation, which allow us to make better decisions leading to a better quality of life.

While these are charming notions, it is evident that merely focusing on the positive is not helpful when we know that these positive messages are by their nature ambiguous. They are ambiguous in the sense that incorporating certain positive traits is not necessarily bad but taken to the extreme can be a deterrent to psychological development and the maturity of identity.

Whether one reads the psychoanalysts or the positive psychologists, a dominant path to happiness is considered to be the love found in the relationships we cultivate. This love is seen in the relationships portrayed in *The Godfather*. The strongest relationships are those among the male characters. If love is too strong a word, then

7

think of it as camaraderie. Fred Gardaphe (2006) calls ethnic male stereotypes presented in film and popular literature "romances," that is, fictitiously embellished accounts or explanations (42). He further states, that "the Italian-American man is the result of the interaction of centuries of Italianate masculinities coming into contact with the variety of masculinities that have developed in the American man" (15).

However you choose to describe these attachments, they are bonds essential to psychological well-being and the development of a positive sense of identity. The group affiliations we choose because of shared values are those that support and enhance individual identity. Yet, love, can and does lead to a loyalty toward the other that diminishes the sense of self and often is detrimental to identity development.

The Godfather gives the audience a glimpse into a particular affiliation that supports male character development. It is a classic buddy movie. Buddy movies have a rich lineage. The 1930s and 1940s gave us Abbott and Costello, Laurel and Hardy, The Dead-End Kids, and' let us not forget, the Hope and Crosby Road Pictures. Through time there have been comedies, dramas, and even musicals — think of *High Society* again with Bing Crosby now partnered with Frank Sinatra. Butch and Sundance made such a good team that *The Sting* followed. More recently, one can classify *Green Book* as a buddy film.

That these films have such popularity and elicit such emotions has to do with the need for those strong male relationships and rests on the concept of homosociality. *The Godfather* is rife with masculine identity tropes that perpetuate the need for homosociality and provides a characterization for how men should be men, largely by creating spaces that are exclusively male. Such images of men bonded toward action are not unique. Masculine enclaves are commonplace in Italian and Italian American culture. From the wild boar hunts in Tuscany to the regional social clubs throughout the United States, there is an opportunity for men to express identity unencumbered by the presence of women, who often serve as the guardians of quotidian social behavior: you need a haircut, put on a tie, and so on. Or, who limit the perceived ability to speak freely especially when the humor leans toward the scatological or profane.

Taking a step back, the expanded use of the term homosociality was first used by Eva Sedgwick to describe male relationships on a continuum from essentially no relationship or no emotionality in a relationship to homosexual relationships. Her work has been within the field of literary criticism, but the concept is a useful one applied to other fields in understanding male relationships. Sedgwick states:

> "Homosocial" is a word occasionally used in history and the social sciences, where it describes social bonds between persons of same sex; it is a neologism, obviously formed by analogy with "homosexual," and just as obviously meant to be distinguished from 'homosexual' . . . to hypothesize the potential unbrokenness of a continuum between homosocial and homosexual — a continuum whose visibility, for man, in our society, is radically disrupted. (1985, 697)

9

Further, Britton argues that a homosociality dominated by the acting out of "macho" stereotypes is in reaction to homophobia (2006).

Theodoros Rakopoulos, who has studied both those actively involved in the mafia in Sicily and those who decide to betray the group, describes the relationship as "dependency in the secretive bonds of violent men" (2020, 686). He argues that homosociality is at work in both circumstances. When the anthropologist Joan Weibel-Orlando asked the squad leader of the boar hunt in Cavarvano if she could attend the boar hunt, she was told, "...*il bosco e bruto* [the forest is an awful place]. It's no place for a woman. We move fast. You a weak woman," unsaid, but clearly inferred] will not be able to keep up with us. It's no place for you [a woman, again unspoken, but understood], especially if you are planning to take your video camera with you" (2008, 163).

Just as the boar hunt is a critical part of the town's economy, so is *The Godfather* about a business enterprise that makes the male relationships even more critical. Edwards reminds us how important the "material, economic and physical foundations of identity and identity politics and indeed power itself" (2006, 103) are found in these circumstances.

In *The Godfather* we see the continuum of male relationships vividly throughout. The film begins in the darkened inner chamber with just a few present, all men, and then expands to the vibrant wedding scenes where there is interaction across gender and age. Subsequently there are varying degrees and depictions of inclusion and exclusion, smaller and larger circles of men, finally ending with not only a return to the inner sanctum of the few, but the door being closed with the woman on the outside.

Which brings us back to homosociality, identity development, and *The Godfather*. To quote Ellis:

"...identification involves both the recognition of self in the image on the screen, a narcissistic identification, and the identification of self with the various positions in the fictional narrative.... Identification is therefore multiple and fractured, a sense of seeing the constituent parts of the spectator's own psych...." (1982, 110)

In *The Godfather* there is an opportunity for the viewer to choose which of the constituent parts fit with their personal narrative. It must be made clear too that homosociality is not in itself a bad thing; being in the sanctuary of one's own chosen gender is reported by many as an important dimension of developing personality identity. In children we see how the configurations move from boys and girls playing together to a separation of genders as puberty emerges to a return of social interaction that later includes sexual implications. Sexual orientation less relevant at the role-playing stages of development as these forays into sexual experimentation lead is to our gender and sexual identity. This process is unfolding constantly in the development of identity as people shift among groups. The exposure to choices widens as the person moves from family to a local community to the broader world of social influence that includes peers, school, media, casual interactions, and traumas experienced. The sway of all media including film and books must not be underestimated in psychological development.

This influence is emphasized by those theoretical perspectives that assert boys are socialized to become men. Film is a way of enacting this socialization and as Edwards points out, "Masculinities now are not so much something possessed as an identity as something marketed, bought — and sold — ...across the world of visual media culture more generally" (2006, 55).

This is the encounter that can and will alter the trajectory of identity development. Film provides intense images of presumed masculinities among other aspects identity; these masculine inclinations are potent in *The Godfather*. These images are then evaluated against the experience of the individual in the world and the individual determines, consciously or sub consciously, which affiliations offer protection and enhancement of the self and emerging psychological identity. Now combine the messages sent in the fantasy world with opportunities for homosociality in the reality of the Italian American experience. The result, in many cases, is a reinforcement of masculine behavior that often excludes women and, in the case of Italian Americans, other ethnic groups to create a cocoon of not only self-protection, but one that builds a wall of disengagement from alternative ways of being.

While this sounds like a completely negative situation, it nonetheless affords a protection to the ego. Everyone chooses group affiliations based upon the defense of the ego and self-identity. The homosocial space for men is a place of retreat from the challenges to the ego in a shared affiliation based on, in the case of a specific gender identification and ethnic identification, common needs and values. The unwillingness or inability to go beyond the man caves of identity is not different from anyone who refuses or cannot break free from the assigned roles and identities of gender or sexuality or ethnicity. Most people choose the comfort of the conventional roles assigned to them and then further defend themselves through their chosen affiliations to those groups that support their choices.

In choosing how to be in the world if one is to maintain the conventions and stereotypes of masculinity, *The Godfather* is a splendid choice. There is protection, loyalty, empathy, love, your buddies cook for you, and bring you cannoli.

WORKS CITED

American Academy of Pediatrics: Committee on Public Education. 2001. "Media Violence." *Pediatrics*, vol. 108, no. 5: 1222+. *Gale Academic OneFile*, link.gale.com/apps/doc/A80221954/AONE? u=cuny_york&sid=bookmark-AONE&xid=741fdbf4. Accessed 21 Feb. 2023.

Bar-On, Reuven. 2001. Emotional intelligence and self-actualization. In Joseph Ciarrochi, Joe Forgas, & John D. Mayer (eds.): *Emotional Intelligence in Everyday Life: A Scientific Iinquiry.* New York: Psychology Press.

Bandura, Albert, Ross, Dorothea, and Ross, Sheila A. 1961. "Transmission of aggression through the imitation of aggressive models." *Journal of Abnormal and Social Psychology.* 63 (3): 575-582.

Bird, Sharon R. 1996. "Men's Club: Homosociality and the Maintenance of Hegemonic Masculinity." *Gender and Society.* Sage Publications Inc., Vol. 10, No. 2: 120-132.

Britton, Dana M. 1990. "Homophobia and Homosociality: An Analysis of Boundary Maintenance." *The Sociological Quarterly* 31, no. 3: 423 — 39. http://www.jstor.org/stable/4120971.

De Stefano, George. 2007. *An Offer We Can't Refuse: The Mafia in the Mind of America.* Farrar, Straus and Giroux.

Edwards, Tim. 2006. *Cultures of Masculinity,* London: Routledge.

Ellis, John. 1982. *Visible Fictions.* London: Routledge.

Gardaphe, Fred. L. 2006. *From Wiseguys to Wise Men: The Gangster and Italian American Masculinities.* New York: Routledge.

Federal Bureau of Investigation. 2023. "Most Wanted." https://www.fbi.gov/wanted/topten Accessed February 15, 2023.

Rakopoulis, Theodoros. 2020. "Two Types of Mafia Dependency: On Making and Unmaking of Mafia Men." *Social Anthropology/Anthropologie Sociale* 28, 3: 686–699.

Rosch, Keri S., Mostofsky Stewart H. 2019. "Development of the frontal lobe." *Handbook of Clinical Neurology.* 163:351-367. doi: 10.1016/B978-0-12-804281-6.00019-7. PMID: 31590741.

Rudolph, Karen D., Troop-Gordon, Wendy, Lambert, Sharon L., & Natsuaki, Misaki N. 2014. "Long-Term Consequences of Pubertal Timing for Youth Depression: Identifying Personal and Contextual Pathways of Risk. *Development and Psychopathology, 26* (4pt2): 1423-1444. doi:10.1017/S0954579414001126

Sedgwick, Eve K. 1985. *Between Men: English literature and Male Homosexual Desire,* New York: Columbia UP.

Joan Weibel-Orlando. 2008. "A Room of (His) Own: Italian and Italian-American Male-bonding Spaces and Homosociality." *The Journal of Men's Studies,* Vol. 16, No. 2: 159-176.

"This one time. This one time I'll let you ask me about my affairs," says Michael to Kay.

Kay witnesses Michael's ascension!

It's not Personal. It's Strictly Education
Sicily Reified in *The Godfather*

CHIARA MAZZUCCHELLI

Many of us find ourselves drawn back to this film time and again, even when it airs late at night in its umpteenth rerun. Those same individuals are likely to have binged on *The Offer*, the 2022 Paramount+ miniseries that explores the development and production of the movie. And when James Caan passed away at the age of 82 in 2022, many of us could not help but think of his character's brutal murder at a tollbooth of the Long Beach Causeway and the heartbreaking words spoken by his father at Bonasera's funeral parlor: "Look how they massacred my boy...". The movie under discussion is *The Godfather*, which celebrated the 50th anniversary of its release last year. Special screenings, symposia, and events were held across the country to mark this occasion, much to the delight of its fans.

One of the key questions that the symposium organized at the John D. Calandra Institute in November 2022 tried to answer was: How does *The Godfather*, fifty years after its original release in 1972, speak to us now? In my contribution, I discussed how I use the movie in class, particularly in my upper-level undergraduate course "From Italy to America" at the University of Central Florida. As its title suggests, the course centers around the Italian American experience, and the assignment topics require the use of primary and secondary sources to introduce students to the history, issues, ideas, and theories of the

Italian ethnic experience in the United States. I believe including *The Godfather* (1972) and *The Godfather Part II* (1974) in my syllabus helps me accomplish all our objectives. This article explores how *The Godfather* saga can serve as a valuable teaching aid for Italian American classes, with a particular focus on the treatment of Sicily in the films. I will especially concentrate on two sequences: the opening sequence featuring young Vito in *Part II* and Michael's trip to Sicily in *The Godfather*. These sequences are presented as pedagogical tools that offer insights into Italian post-Unification history, the diasporic experience, and narratives of longing and belonging. They also provide answers to common questions that my students have about Sicily and the Mafia.

Let me state at the outset that while I am among those who believe that *The Godfather* is a cinematic masterpiece, I also acknowledge it may not be a classic that everyone celebrates. Because of its intrinsically ethnic character and controversial themes, *The Godfather* continues to cause very intense responses in favor or against its articulation of the Italian American experience. Critic John Paul Russo is right to point out that the Italian American "villain-heroes and their shadowy cohorts have been made to [...] elicit varied reactions (identification, anger, recrimination, rejection). The only reaction absent seems to be neutrality" (434). For instance, Mario Cuomo, the late three-term Governor of New York State, spent his entire life fighting the "ugly stereotype" that threatened to hurt his career and tarnished the reputation of millions of honest and hard-working Italian Americans (Schmalz, "Cuomo Condemns"). Cuomo held strong opinions against *The God-*

father and admitted to watching the movie for the first time in his life in 2013 (Roberts, "Mario Cuomo")! The son of Italian immigrants from Queens, Cuomo was critical of the romanticized portrayal of Italian Americans as gangsters in *The Godfather*, which he believed cast a shadow over an entire ethnic group. Criticism of Puzo and Coppola's saga ran in the Cuomo family. When in 2019, Chris Cuomo, Mario's youngest son and brother of New York Governor Andrew, was taunted by a conservative protester with a *Godfather* reference, the CNN anchor responded with obvious anger, sparking a debate about ethnic slurs and defamation that the media dubbed "Fredogate" (Gold, "CNN's Chris Cuomo"). The Cuomos' views are shared by many Italian Americans, offended by the demeaning images circulated by mainstream media that portray them as gangsters, violent brutes, or thugs.

These claims are, admittedly, not without merit. In fact, in my twenty years of teaching Italian in the United States, I have noticed that Sicily, my birthplace, occupies almost legendary status in the minds of my students due, in part, to the lasting influence of *The Godfather*. While my students don't know much about Sicily, most of their questions revolve around the "secret society" that the movie portrays. Almost every semester I am asked to talk about the Mafia in at least one of my classes, and occasionally, a particularly ambitious student will prepare a fifteen-minute presentation on the history of the Mafia from its origins to the present day. Educators must fulfill the responsibilities of their job and when faced with students' interest, they must do what is necessary: that is, educate. There is more than one reason why I include *The Godfather* in my syllabus, but this is the main reason.

The Godfather is undeniably one of the most significant cultural works produced in American history over the past fifty years. Regardless of our personal feelings towards it — whether we are drawn in by the story or troubled by its portrayal of Italian Americans as gangsters — Puzo's novel and Coppola's films help us gain a deeper understanding of the complexities, promises, and shortcomings of this country. In fact, *The Godfather* offers valuable lessons on U.S. history, cultural events, and politics. The saga also sheds light on the underlying reasons behind the Great Migration from Italy to the United States that occurred at the turn of the 20th century. Finally, in terms of Sicily, it can be argued that no work has done more to put the island on the world map (metaphorically speaking) than *The Godfather*. Ever since the publication of Puzo's novel in 1969, which quickly became a bestseller, and even more so after Coppola's film adaptation a few years later — which paved the way for the mobster culture industry that followed — Sicily has captured a powerful hold on the American imagination.[1] In his 2017 book *Non c'è più la Sicilia di una volta*, Italian journalist Gaetano Savatteri pointed out that

---

[1] For an analysis of the gangster figure in American culture particularly as it relates to gender roles and masculinity, see Fred Gardaphe's *From Wiseguys to Wisemen* (2006). It is important to note that, as Anthony Tamburri argues in his article "Italian Americans and Television," Puzo and Coppola's saga were preceded not only by a number of movies but also TV series that famously portrayed Italian Americans as gangsters, among which so-called "cops and wops" TV shows like the American crime drama *The Untouchables* (1959-1963).

Sicily has a projection larger than itself. There are places in Italy whose image is bigger than reality. To use marketing language, one could say these places have a very strong *brand* recognition, that is a famous and well-known trademark (like, for instance, Ferrari or Coca-Cola). (ix; my translation).

While Rome boasts a rich history and architecture, Florence has art treasures, and Venice features its picturesque canals and gondolas; there is also Sicily, and its association with the Mafia. It would be naïve to ignore the significant impact that Puzo and Coppola's masterful treatment of the subject had on the global popularization of the Mafia as a social phenomenon specifically associated with Sicilian culture. We also cannot downplay the harm caused by the widespread dissemination of these representations, which negatively affect the perception of an entire ethnic group by others and, also, their self-perception as ethnic Americans. In a 2002 article on cinematographic representations of Italian Americans in the United States, Ben Lawton lamented that a quick search of the Internet Movie Data Base for movies that include "Mafia" in the title confirmed that Italian Americans have been overwhelmingly represented as violent criminals in American cinema. "The number of films that deal with organized crime and that either state or imply that it is comprised of Italian Americans is virtually endless," Lawton noted, while "there is absolutely no reasonable correlation between the extremely limited involvement of Italian Americans with organized crime and the pandemic depiction of this alleged involvement in the media" (Lawton, 71-72).[2] We can safely assume that in the twenty years since Lawton's IMDB search the number of movies on and about the Mafia has gone up, and while Italy and the United States have made significant progress in the fight against organized crime and Mafia-related activities, it appears that the popular culture industry is reluctant to let go of financially successful formulas from the past.[3]

However, it is important to recognize that the impact of these representations is cumulative, in the sense that *The Godfather* alone is clearly not solely responsible for the consolidation of the equation 'Sicily + Italy + Italian America = Mafia.' Examining the cultural production of a highly successful Hollywood genre that shapes national conversations and important debates within the Italian American community is an effective way to encourage students to think critically and reason through complex issues presented in different texts. My "From Italy to Ameri-

[2] In 1997, William Dal Cerro compiled a list of what he termed "Ital-bashing" Hollywood movies, amounting to "450 titles which have created a cultural 'Berlin Wall' of Italian stereotyping" (10). According to Dal Cerro's estimates, approximately 12% of movies produced in Hollywood between 1931 and 1997 portrayed Italians as "positive characters," while the vast majority depicted them as "mob characters" (52%) or "boors, buffoons, bigots" (36%).
[3] The most recent iteration delivered by Hollywood is *Mafia Mamma*, directed by Catherine Harwicke, which opened in theaters on April 14, 2023. The plot involves an all-American and college-educated suburban mom (Toni Collette) who ends up taking the reins of her late grandfather's Mafia family. In the trailer, the protagonist admits having never watched *The Godfather*, causing the horror of her *consigliere* (Monica Bellucci) and the hitmen. An upcoming gangster film with Robert De Niro playing the roles of noted Mafia bosses Vito Genovese and Frank Costello is *Wise Guys*, written by Nicholas Pileggi and directed by Barry Levinson, which is scheduled to be released in February of 2024.

ca" class is one of the upper-level undergraduate courses we offer to students pursuing an Italian Minor at the University of Central Florida and one of the very few we offer in English. The course brings together critical, theoretical, literary, and cinematic texts to gain a deeper understanding of discourses on Italian American identities and the immigrant experience. The unit that I dedicate to *The Godfather* saga usually lasts two (out of fifteen) weeks and is the third unit in the course. To ensure students have a clear understanding of the films, I ask them to watch the first two installments in the saga on their own for knowledge and comprehension so that class time is spent on lectures and in-depth discussions based on the assigned readings, and to address questions on any aspect of the filmic and critical texts. Although none of the students enrolled in this class in Spring '22 had ever watched the movie(s) before, they were, of course, familiar with the trope of the Italian American gangster. By pairing the films with critical readings, students are able to better understand the broader historical and cultural significance of *The Godfather* and to engage critically with it.

Noteworthy is that while in the pre-watching stage my Spring '22 students perceived *The Godfather* as a quintessential Italian American narrative, after watching the films, many of them highlighted the prominent role that Sicily plays in the story. Some of them raised questions about whether it is fair to "judge" an entire ethnic group based solely on the actions of individuals from one region. These questions were addressed through assigned readings, including Werner Sollors' "Foreword" to his 1996 book *Theories of Ethnicity* and other texts that explore the content and boundaries of ethnic identities, such as the section entitled "Ethnic Semiosis" in Chris Messenger's *The Godfather and American Culture.*

My students' questions are, in fact, appropriate since Sicily and its culture are at the core of Coppola's saga. The opening sequence of Connie Corleone's wedding is a great example of the movie's use of Sicilian culture with its inclusion of traditional music, dance, and, famously, the bawdy Sicilian song *A luna mezz'u mari* sung by Mama Corleone. The use of Sicilian dialect in the dialogues also adds to the authenticity of the representation, and many now–famous quotes include Sicilian traditions or "messages" that have now entered the common parlance of many different languages.

One such instance occurs during Connie's wedding. When supplicants flood Don Corleone's office asking for help to settle various disputes, Tom Hagen explains to his wife, "It's part of the wedding: No Sicilian can refuse any request on his daughter's wedding day," a magnanimity that is, of course, not free of entanglements since the Don expects loyalty and, possibly, a favor in return. The famous package of Luca Brasi's bulletproof-vest-wrapped fish is another prime example of how some pillars of Sicilian Mafia culture are intricately woven into *The Godfather* saga. In the aftermath of the assassination attempt on the Don and the kidnapping of Tom Hagen, the family hunkers down at the Long Island compound to decide on the best course of action to exact revenge on Virgil "The Turk" Sollozzo and the Tattaglia family, who are behind the attack. They all wonder where the Don's loyal hitman Luca Brasi is when the answer arrives in the form of a brown package delivered to Sonny by Tessio: "What the hell is this?" Sonny asks, puzzled by its content, "It's a Sicilian message," Clemenza explains, "It means Luca Brasi sleeps with the fishes."[4] This scene encapsulates in a memorable way the Sicilian Mafia concepts of *omertà*, the code of silence (Luca Brasi is now silent as a fish and the Corleones too should keep quiet about his death) and *vendetta* (Brasi's death by murder caused by his attempt to fool Sollozzo).

Finally, a discussion on iconic symbols of Sicily, which are now indelibly etched in our collective consciousness thanks in part to *The Godfather*, would be incomplete without mentioning *cannolis*. The famous Sicilian ricotta-filled pastry is the focal point the murder of Paulie, the Don's bodyguard who is suspected of betraying his boss by calling in sick on the day of the attempted murder. It does not take long for Sonny and Clemenza to figure out that "Paulie sold out the old man," and, thus, his fate is sealed. But just before Clemenza gets into the car that will ultimately be Paulie's final ride, his wife warns him: "Don't forget the cannoli!" After Paulie is shot inside the car on the side of the road, Clemenza famously gives his hitman Rocco the following instructions: "Leave the gun, take the cannoli," thus outlining the steps and

---

[4] American novelist Herman Melville famously conveyed the same image in his 1851 *Moby-Dick*, where second mate Stubb philosophizes as follows: "when Aquarius, or the Water-bearer, pours out his whole deluge and drowns us; and *to wind up with Pisces, or the Fishes, we sleep*" (430, my emphasis). But while "Call me Ishmael" is now one of the most famous incipits in the history of world's literature, Melville will have to concede to Puzo and Coppola when it comes to "sleeping with the fishes."

priorities of a murder Sicilian-style.[5] *The Godfather* trilogy is steeped in Sicilian culture from start to finish, with the island serving as the common thread that ties multiple generations —including Vito's father and Michael's son — together. These and other references to Sicilian traditions and customs have played a significant role in the films' enduring popularity and lasting influence.

It all starts with Don Vito Corleone, the patriarch whose name symbolizes his Sicilian heritage. In *Part II*, the second film of the trilogy, we discover that the Don's original name was Vito Andolini and that he hailed from the town of Corleone. His first name, Vito, is derived from the Latin word *vita*, meaning "life." Upon arriving at Ellis Island, an immigration official changed his last name to that of his birthplace. In sum, due to a clerical error, Vito Andolini becomes the flagbearer of life in Corleone as transplanted to the United States. His nickname, the Don, from the Latin *dominus*, "Lord," is an honorific title that signifies power in both secular and religious contexts. In Italy, it was often used to refer to priests and noblemen (as in the parish priest Don Abbondio and the local baron Don Rodrigo in Alessandro Manzoni's historical novel *The Betrothed*). In Sicily, though, the title "Don" is also used as a sign of respect when addressing older and presumably wiser individuals, and by (perverted) extension, to Mafia bosses. In *The Godfather*, Don Vito Corleone is the larger-than-life father, grandfather,

---

[5] If we want to include *Part III* in this discussion, we should also mention the famous poisoned cannoli that Connie gifts Don Altobello on his 80th birthday and that kills him silently during a performance at the Teatro Massimo in Palermo.

and godfather figure, often referred to as "the" godfather. "Because he is the center of the world he has re-created in America," Fred Gardaphe explains, the Don "is like God who makes all things, good and evil, and is the force that is cursed as it is praised by those who live under his dominion" (*Italian Signs*, 95). My students often remark on the God-like qualities of Don Vito, especially his power, of course, and, more interestingly, his perceived benevolence toward those in need. It is important to problematize this initial reaction and delve into the multiple layers of representations, perceptions, and meanings at play. By engaging in critical reflections on the interaction between a text and its reception, we can empower students to approach representations, ideas, and concepts in more cautious ways.

To achieve these objectives, I employ a range of teaching methods, including readings, lectures, class discussion, writing assignments, and close textual analyses. While students are expected to watch the movies on their own, in class we focus on two specific sequences, which are particularly important for the purpose of understanding the role Sicily and Sicilian culture play in the movies. The first of these is the opening flashback in the first sequel, *The Godfather Part II*, which is also chronologically the beginning of the entire saga.

THE FATHER

The sequence opens with a somber funeral in the year 1901 in the small town of Corleone, in the province of Palermo. Nine-year old Vito Andolini, his mother, and a few family members and friends follow the coffin of Vito's

27

father through a recognizably west-coast Sicilian land-scape: barren countryside, rocky terrain, and small hillside towns in the background. The death by murder of Vito's father is made even more tragic by the killing, during the funeral, of Vito's fourteen-year-old brother Paolo, who was seeking revenge against their father's assassin, the local Mafia chieftain Don Ciccio. In just a few scenes, the screenwriters Puzo and Coppola transport us back to turn-of-the-twentieth century Sicily, providing insights into its history, culture, and economy that prove useful for a solid lesson plan.

The likes of Don Ciccio, in fact, had been the targets of Sicilian uprisings since before the Unification of Italy. Following the official annexation of the island to the newly formed Kingdom of Italy in 1860, peasants had hoped for much-needed land reforms to alleviate the burden imposed on them by landowners. However, when Garibaldi failed to align himself with the peasantry against the old feudal ruling class, a series of insurrections began in various towns, most notably Bronte, in the province of Catania. Sicilian writer Giovanni Verga, who belonged to the landowning elite, depicted the facts of Bronte in the pressing prose of his 1882 *novella* "Liberty" with a paternalistic and conservative perspective on issues of class inequalities that also informs his most famous novel, *I Malavoglia*. In Verga's short story, the different styles of hats worn by the peasants and the gentry came to symbolize the two sides of the class and social conflicts in late 19th and early 20th century Sicily, i.e., *berretti* vs. *cappelli*:

Like the sea in storm. The crowd foamed and swayed in
front of the club of the gentry [*galantuomini*], and outside the Town Hall, and on the steps of the church — a
sea of white stocking-caps [*berrette bianche*], axes and
sickles glittering. Then they burst into the little street
[...] And blood smoked and went drunk. Sickles, hands,
rags, stones, everything red with blood! *The gentry! The
hat-folks!* [*Ai galantuomi! Ai Cappelli!*] Kill them all!
Kill them all! Down with the *hat-folks*! (197-198)

As we know, the Bronte riots were repressed, and "order"
was eventually restored by Nino Bixio. However, social un-
rest was growing, and Sicilian peasants finally organized
in the *fasci siciliani*, a popular movement of democratic
and socialist inspiration that spread around the island between 1888 and 1894. The *fasci* provided an important social and political platform for Sicilian farmers, aimed to
improve the living conditions of the peasants and to challenge the power of local landowners and the Mafia.

In his 1977 study *I fasci siciliani,* historian Francesco
Renda points out that, "the leading elements in the form-
ative process of the organization are not the workers nor
the artisans, but the farmers. The center of gravity moves
from the city to the countryside" (10; my translation). The
town of Corleone was a hotbed of protests during this period. Following the issuance of new policies that did not
please the *fasci*, in August of 1893, the movement organized in Corleone the first mass farmers' strike in Italian
history. From there, the protest quickly spread across the
island but, once again, the soldiers met the farmers' de-
mands with bullets. In an ironic and cruel twist of destiny,

it was a Sicilian, Francesco Crispi, the newly appointed Prime Minister of Italy, who decided to repress the *fasci* by sending an army of forty thousand soldiers to the island. The history of the *fasci siciliani* can be considered concluded with the proclamation of the state of siege throughout Sicily in January of 1894.

Don Ciccio is depicted as a *cappeddu*, one of the hat-folks who wielded power in Sicily at the turn of twentieth century. He lives in a gated baronial estate, sporting suspenders over a white shirt and a gold Albert watch chain on his vest. He sips his drink with his pinky sticking out, embodying the typical image of a powerful and arrogant man. The portrayal of Don Ciccio as the clear villain in *Part II* leaves no room for ambiguity. He is the obvious antagonist in the story, and his equivalents in Sicily were the ones who controlled the lives of peasants, demanding their services and loyalty. After losing her husband and oldest son, Vito's mother pleads with Don Ciccio to spare her young boy's life since, she claims, Vito poses no threat to the boss since he is *fissa* (dimwitted and weak). When Don Ciccio refuses and threatens the boy's life, the mother sacrifices herself to allow her son to escape, using a knife to threaten the boss before being killed by a shotgun blast.

In less than five minutes of screen time, the opening sequence of *Part II* accomplishes the remarkable feat of condensing fifty plus years of Sicilian social and economic history, while also contextualizing the protagonist's experience. This, in turn, helps us better understand some of the social and economic dynamics that underpin the Sicilian migration to and diasporic experience in the United

States. With the help of some *paesani*, Vito is able to board a ship bound to New York. One of the most memorable scenes in the movie involves the arrival at the New York harbor, with hundreds of passengers huddled together on the deck staring with awe at the Statue of Liberty as the ship glides past it. The sight of the "American Madonna," a symbol of hope and freedom, is a powerful image that evokes the dreams and aspirations of millions of people who came to America seeking a better life. In the great hall of Ellis Island, young Vito, along with hundreds of other immigrants from various countries, is processed by Immigration officers. The boy's transformation from Vito Andolini to Vito Corleone signifies the change of an immigrant's identity to embrace a new life in a foreign land. The boy's personal story becomes a parable —albeit a particularly striking and violent one — for the larger history of emigration from Sicily to the United States.

Emigration played a significant role in the lives of Sicilians throughout the 20th century. The island's finite geography and limited resources contributed to a lack of economies of scale leading to a decline of standard of living and quality of life, therefore encouraging emigration. But this Malthusian reading alone does not fully capture the complexities of Sicilian emigration. Since the Unification of Italy, in fact, these challenges, combined with the newborn state's inability to effectively address the unique realities of the Italian South, caused Sicily — and the entire *Mezzogiorno*, for that matter — to experience periods of intense emigration.

In the early 1900s, Sicily underwent a massive displacement of its people to the United States similar to the mass emigration movements of two other islands: Ireland during the second half of the nineteenth century and Puerto Rico since World War II. Interestingly, Sicily was, chronologically speaking, among the last regions of Italy to join the mass emigration trend that changed the profile of the new-born country starting in 1876.[6] However, Sicily caught up with other regions in terms of numbers, particularly during the period from 1901 to 1914. According to historian Luigi Arcuri Di Marco, during the period from 1876 to 1900, Sicilians accounted for only 7.7% of Italy's total emigrants. Between 1901 and 1914, though, they represented no less than 20.8% of the total. In fact, during the same period, about two-thirds of the total emigration from Italy between 1876 and 1925 occurred. In 1913, over 146,000 people left Sicily, which was a record number not matched by any other Italian region in history. In terms of destinations, over a period of fifty years, almost 90% of the movements from Sicily were transoceanic. Between 1876 and 1925, approximately 1.5 million Sicilians left the island, with 77% of them directed to the United States. These figures are particularly significant when we take into account that at the beginning of the 20th century, the population of Sicily was only 3.5 million.

After sharing these numbers with my students in my Spring '22 "From Italy to America" course, their reactions ranged from surprise to understanding. Although several of them had personal connections to Sicilian heritage or family members and friends who did, none of them had

---

[6] 1876 was the year when Italy began recording comprehensive emigration statistics and reliable data on migration and, therefore, it has become the starting point of what is now known as the Great Emigration.

realized the extent of the migratory phenomenon. The numbers were much larger than they suspected. Perhaps unsurprisingly, all of my students showed an understanding of the intricate mechanisms of migratory patterns. This might be due to the composition of our student body, which includes 49% minorities and 28.2% Hispanic students out of the more than 68,000 students enrolled at the University of Central Florida. The inherent diversity in backgrounds, personal stories, and perspectives of our students allowed for an engaging discussion in class on immigration and ethnicity, drawing parallels between the Italian American experience and the experiences of other ethnic groups.

Returning to our story, or rather, our lesson plan, Vito arrives in New York alone, but he has no trouble finding fellow *paesani* around Mulberry Street. Under Coppola's direction, New York's Little Italy is a vivid representation of a turn-of-twentieth-century Italian *colonia*, and a unique visual depiction of that time and place. In contrast to Jacob Riis' famous raw portrayals of the tenements in *How the Other Half Lives*, the Italian immigrant community in New York is represented in much warmer tones in Coppola's film. I did, however, show my students a selection of Riis' photographs to provide them with a necessary "re-grounding" and a reminder of one of the most notable examples of romanticization of bygone (ethnic) days in the saga.

The Little Italy where Vito Andolini arrives is not the problematic slum where poverty and crime festered, which raised the eyebrows of sociologists, politicians, and Americans who feared the intrusion of a premodern and predominantly peasant civilization in "their" country. In *The Godfather*, Mulberry Street is a mosaic of sounds, sights, and people that reflect the director's desire to showcase his ethnic heritage in his film. It is maybe closer to the Italian enclave described in Italian ethnographer Amy Bernardy's 1911 *America vissuta*, with streets packed with "types, accents, general intonation of the environment in which the American face and voice is an exception," alive with the hustle and bustle of *grosserie*, carts, and street peddlers speaking various Southern Italian dialects.[7] Coppola's Little Italy is first and foremost a neighborhood, a close-knit community of people who formed a web of social and economic relations. It was this network of human relationships that allowed the nine-year old Vito Andolini to not only survive in America but also, eventually, albeit through questionable means, to move "up" from his humble beginnings in Mulberry Street to a mansion on Long Island. Little Italy is a place that many Americans of Italian descent, who by 1972 had achieved a middle-class suburban lifestyle, would recognize as their own. Non-Italians too can appreciate the sense of unity and the feeling of hope it inspires. For my twenty-year old UCF students, many of whom are first-generation Americans and the first in their

---

[7] Bernardy, *America*, 306-307 (my translation). During the first decades of the 20th century, Bernardy famously undertook an analysis of the living and moral conditions of Italian immigrants of the Little Italies, an assignment that she received from the Italian *Commissariato Generale dell'Emigrazione*, a government agency founded in 1910 with the goal of overseeing and arranging all matters related to the emigration of Italian nationals abroad. Bernardy's study resulted in several publications, among which the 1911 *America vissuta*, in which she focused on the "Piccola Italia" of Boston's North End.

families to attend college, Coppola's Little Italy represents a sense of purpose, determination, and courage. In short, it serves as a visual and metaphorical return to the roots for millions of viewers.

Let's now shift our attention from Vito's early life in New York to his son Michael's storyline in Sicily.

THE SON

It goes without saying that *The Godfather* is first and foremost the story of a family. The significance of family in Italian American culture has received a lot of scholarly attention in the fields of Italian and Italian American studies. In fact, family is considered one of the four main topoi — or "F" words — in both fields of studies, alongside Food, Fashion, and Football. In one of her perceptive essays, Joanne Ruvoli pointed out that, "family issues and family values appear in most major studies of Italian American literature, film, history, psychology, and sociology. Fictional families like the Corleones and the Sopranos are as real to mainstream society as the Kennedys, the Bushes or the Clintons" (404). The Corleones are a quintessential Italian American family. But this family has more to it than meets the eye.

In his Introduction to *The Godfather Notebook*, Francis Ford Coppola famously stated that in his mind, *The Godfather* was "a story that was a metaphor for American capitalism in the tale of a great king with three sons: the oldest was given his passion and aggressiveness, the second his sweet nature and childlike qualities, and the third his intelligence, cunning, and coldness" (24). The Corleones hold mythical stature similar to royalty. Coppola highlights the qualities the three sons inherited from their father, but it is important to consider what they did not inherit from him. Don Vito rules with a sense of honor, instilling both fear and respect in those around him. He emphasizes the importance of being a man, meaning, strong and tough, while also being a family man. Finally, he rules with discretion and composure. We know Sonny possesses great intimidation skills but lacks composure and is known for being hotheaded, a trait that, eventually, gets him killed. On the other hand, Fredo, Vito Corleone's middle son, lacks the intelligence and fear-inducing potential of the Don, which results in him taking a backseat to his younger brother Michael, who takes over their father's empire. Fredo is the weakest link in the family, which explains — but does not excuse, of course — Chris Cuomo's violent reaction to being called a Fredo, as mentioned earlier, and the anchor's claim that being called a "Fredo" is the Italian American equivalent of "the N-word." In contrast to his brothers, Michael seems to possess all his father's qualities. He is an honorable and brave man, having earned the badge of "war hero" during his time in the Army. He is family-oriented, composed, overall, a very promising heir to the Corleone throne. There is only one catch: he wants no part in the family business. However, with the Don incapacitated and a looming war in the horizon, Michael is forced to step up and take on a role in the Family business. As Gardaphe points out in his *Italian Signs*:

> Up to this point, Michael has been as innocent as the women in the Corleone clan. He has been kept out of the family business and has had a hero's upbringing,

36

the American equivalent of an aristocrat's education, with knightly training in the marines through which he achieves heroism during the war. His military service is part of his attempt to Americanize himself. It represents loyalty to a power that is not Sicilian and rebellion to his father's wishes. (92)

But despite being forced into the family business due to circumstances beyond his control — or the Sicilian notion of *destinu* — Michael does not share his family's worldview. He proudly rejects the cultural values that have shaped his father's life and, by extension, his family. For this second-generation Sicilian American to gain a better understanding and, maybe, acceptance of his heritage, education is key. And what better place to learn than Sicily itself, where he goes to hide out after gunning down Sollozzo and Captain McClusky?

The events depicted in the sequence in question occur about forty-five years after Vito's sequence in *Part II*, which we analyzed earlier. The setting is post-World War II Sicily, and the year is roughly 1946-1947. As before, this sequence too takes place in the traditional Sicilian countryside. The scene is painted with the burnt yellow of the wheat fields, sheep grazing, olive trees, hills in the background, and a few cube-like stone houses scattered around.

At the beginning of the sequence, Michael is seen walking with his two Sicilian bodyguards, Fabrizio and Calo. All three men are wearing a *coppola*, or *birritta*, the flat cap typically worn by peasants in Sicily. This detail, as we discussed earlier, further establishes Michael's connection to the Andolini/Corleone lineage. After a long hike, the three finally arrive in Corleone, the Don's hometown. In his 2004 study *Cosa Nostra: A History of the Sicilian Mafia*, John Dickie labels the Sicilian sequence of *The Godfather* as "undeniably crass" (259). The British historian specifically points to a scene in which Michael, realizing the town looks deserted, wonders where all the men have gone: "Unni sunu i masculi?", to which one of his bodyguards replies: "sono morti tutti per vendetta." Dickie adds: "He speaks the word [vendetta] as if it meant some unholy force of nature, a variant of the black Death that mows down only Sicilian men" (259). Discussing the same scene, Gardaphe points out that "the reality would be that they all left looking for work in Germany and other more industrialized areas of Europe" (*From Wiseguys*, 39). Although the critic is correct to highlight the impact of emigration in the desertion of Sicilian men, he would still have to agree with the historian, who noted that the murder rate in Corleone during that period was "strikingly high." "These were the years," Dickie continues, "of the Mafia's resurgence and of its brutal response to renewed peasant militancy" (260). In fact, if we look closely, we can see a Communist Party street-poster pasted on a wall next to a death notice in one of the frames.

Although Corleone developed a reputation as a Mafia hotbed during the '70s and '80s, during the late 1940s the notorious Mafia boss Luciano Liggio committed a political killing by murdering the activist and trade union leader Placido Rizzotto in the town. Liggio went on to become the leader of *il club dei corleonesi* Mafia clan, which included some of the most feared and powerful mafiosi, such as Leonardo Provenzano, Leoluca Bagarella, and Totò Riina. The latter gained notoriety for ordering the *attentatuni* of 1992, which took the lives of anti-Mafia judges Giovanni Falcone and Paolo Borsellino, along with Falcone's wife and several police officers.

While in Sicily, Michael tries to escape his past and leave the attempt on his father's life, the murder of Sollozzo and McClusky, and the Mafia war that is currently underway behind him. He embraces the traditional Sicilian way of life and falls in love with a local girl, Apollonia. He is determined to do things the right way, that is, the Sicilian way. His desire to assimilate into Sicilian culture is evident in his approach to courtship. Complying with local customs, he speaks to the girl's father and meets her family before pursuing a relationship. When he goes on long walks with Apollonia, he does so under the watchful eyes of a crowd of older women who chaperone the couple. Eventually, he marries her in a traditional Sicilian ceremony. However, his romantic Sicilian dream is cut short when Apollonia is killed in a car explosion that was meant to kill him. This tragedy, coupled with Sonny's brutal execution back in New York, underscores the ruthless reality of the violent world Michael had hoped so desperately to escape. The Don's son comes to the realization that leaving behind his family's criminal lifestyle is not possible, after all. In a discussion on masculinity in *The Godfather*, Gardaphe notes: "The education Michael receives during his exile in Sicily enables him to take command of his father's kingdom in the United States and ruthlessly rule it in an Old-World manner" (*From Wiseguys*, 37). Michael's Sicilian interlude is a turning point as he realizes he must embrace his family's legacy to confront his enemies. Michael's time in Sicily prepares him to lead the Corleone family with an iron fist.

Both sequences that we analyzed in this essay provide a glimpse into the Italian American ethnic experience and, at the same time, highlight various issues that the community faced throughout the 20th century. The first sequence, which focuses on Vito Corleone's youth in Sicily and emigration to the United States, depicts the struggles of early Italian immigrants in America and their challenges when trying to make a better living for themselves and their families. It also shows how an individual's ethnic identity can be shaped by their cultural background and experiences. The second sequence, which features Michael Corleone hiding out in Sicily, delves into the complexities of the dilemma of a second-generation ethnic torn between his American identity and his Sicilian roots.

As a saga about the Sicilian ethnic experience in the United States, Puzo and Coppola's *The Godfather* can be read as a cautionary tale of the challenges faced by immigrants in America, particularly those from Sicily, as they strive to achieve social acceptance and economic success. Vito's choice to resort to the violent methods of the Mafia can be seen as a reflection of the historically justified lack of trust in the government's ability to redress economic and social inequalities. However, unlike Vito's decision, Michael's choice to follow in his father's footsteps cannot be justified by the same reasons. This was a point of contention among my students, as they struggled to reconcile Michael's actions with his identity as an "American." During class discussions, they raised thought-provoking questions about whether Michael's acceptance of his *destinu* was truly inevitable. After all, in *Part II*, they pointed out, he finally shows that he is unable to cope with the inner conflicts arising from his choice to embrace violence and eventually degenerates into a dysfunctional state.[8]

My students came to the conclusion that *The Godfather* is, in fact, a condemnation of organized crime, more than a romanticization of it. The films show that involvement in organized crime can only result in social and personal failure and that violence takes a massive toll on the immigrant's life but also on their family. They also pointed out that as much as the films purport to be about family and the importance of keeping it together, in the end, as Ruvoli also argues, "to avenge the Corleone family empire, newly ascended Michael murders the heads of the other five families in the climactic scenes of *Godfather I*, but even within his family, brothers and brothers-in-laws attempt and ultimately kill each other in defense of their individual family interests," thus leaving us to wonder whether the concept of "family" for Italian Americans has a universal value and, if it doesn't, where does the allegiance start and where does it end (411). These and other class discussions on relevant topics indicated that several

---

[8] As John Paul Russo explains, "the viewer might not deplore [Michael's] elimination of evil bosses at the end of *Godfather I*, as they are no worse than he is, but he has killed or harmed innocent people, compromised his family, and lied cruelly to his wife (...). He has located a conspirator in his brother-in-law Carlo and has him garroted; and Tessio has double-crossed him and has paid the price. Fredo is falling victim to the Las Vegas high life and will soon betray him. Business and family unity show signs of cracking, and Michael's face begins to wear an expression of impassivity and gloom that characterize him in *Godfather II*" (451).

of the primary objectives of our course were met. By delving into the story, the context it portrays, and themes it explores, my students learn to cultivate critical thinking skills and contemplate alternative interpretations rather than simply accepting prevailing ones.

CONCLUSION: THE UNHOLY GHOST

The Godfather and *The Godfather Part II* are just the points of departure for the unit I put together in my "From Italy to America" course and, as I mentioned earlier, required reading assignments include theoretical essays to ground a discussion on the impact of stereotypes as well as several critical interpretations of *The Godfather*. While *The Godfather* saga is, for obvious reasons, inextricably linked to the Mafia, organized crime is certainly one of the themes discussed but not the centerpiece of the module, let alone of the entire course.[9] The class emphasizes learning about the history of emigration, the literature of Italian Americans and popular cinematic texts on the Italian American experience, notions of ethnic identities and assimilation, the role of Catholicism in Italian American culture, gender and class issues, prejudices, and stereotypes. Throughout the course, we explore topics that pertain to the ethnic experience in the United

---

[9] This specific course explores the Italian American experience as a whole. However, in American colleges it is not uncommon to find courses solely dedicated to exploring the portrayal of the Mafia in classic Italian and Hollywood films. Jacqueline Reich was among the first to undertake the task of curating such a course at UC Berkeley in the early 1990s. In her essay titled "Godfathers, Goodfellas and Madonnas," published in *Voices in Italian Americana* in 1993, Reich detailed her pedagogical approach in developing this captivating course.

States, regardless of the particular group involved. In fact, the topics we cover in this course are as relevant to my fourth-generation Italian American students who want to learn more about their heritage as they are to my Hispanic students who have only recently arrived in the United States. Analyzing *The Godfather* in class is a process of discovery and self-discovery for all of them.

Italian Studies film scholar Peter Bondanella argued that

> [n]egative stereotypes exist in the representation of Hollywood Italians, but the quality of so many of the great films depicting Hollywood Italians is so high that for many such films (*The Godfather* is the best example) it is impossible to reject these great works as merely perpetuating stereotypes, just as it is impossible to ignore the literary values of such Shakespeare plays as *Othello* and *The Merchant of Venice* on the grounds that there are politically incorrect expressions of racial or religious prejudice. (219)

As educators, it is not our role to shy away from sensitive and controversial topics that may make us or our community uncomfortable, nor can we choose to remain silent about one of the most influential portrayals of Italian Americans on screen, in the hope that new generations will ignore its existence. Examining cultural issues and addressing painful experiences is crucial for our students' learning and growth. It is also a necessary conversation to have within our community. In short, the educational opportunities offered by *The Godfather* are plentiful, making it an offer I can't refuse.

WORKS CITED

Bernardy, Amy A. 1911. *America vissuta.* Torino: Fratelli Bocca Editori.

Bondanella, Peter. 2010. "Palookas, Romeos, and Wise Guys: Italian Americans in Hollywood." In *Teaching Italian American Literature, Film, and Popular Culture*, edited by Edvige Giunta and Kathleen Zamboni McCormick, 217-222. New York: The Modern Language Association of America.

Coppola, Francis Ford, Director. 1972. *The Godfather.* Paramount Pictures.

Coppola, Francis Ford, Director. 1974. *The Godfather Part II.* Paramount Pictures.

Coppola, Francis Ford. 2016. *The Godfather Notebook.* New York: Regan Arts.

Dal Cerro, William. 1997. "Hollywood versus Italians: Them – 400; Us – 50." *The Italic Way* 27: 10-32.

Di Marco, Arcuri Luigi. 1996. "L'emigrazione siciliana all'estero nel cinquantennio 1876-1925." *Annali del Mezzogiorno* VI: 169-232.

Dickie, John. 2004. *Cosa Nostra: A History of the Sicilian Mafia.* New York: Palgrave.

Gardaphe, Fred. 2006. *From Wiseguy to Wisemen. The Gangster and Italian American Masculinities.* New York: Routledge.

Gardaphe, Fred. 1996. *Italian Signs, American Streets. The Evolution of Italian American Narrative.* Durham: Duke UP.

Gold, Michael. 2019. "CNN's Chris Cuomo Threatens Man Who Called Him 'Fredo'." *New York Times*, Aug. 13. https://www.nytimes.com/2019/08/13/nyregion/fredo-cuomo-video.html.

Harwicke, Catherine, Director. 2023. *Mafia Mamma.* New Sparta Production.

Lawton, Ben. 2002. "The Mafia and the Movies: Why is Italian American Synonymous with Organized Crime?" In *Screening*

Ethnicity, edited by Anna Camaiti Hostert and Anthony Julian Tamburri, 69-95. Boca Raton: Bordighera P.

Levinson, Barry, Director. 2024 (scheduled release). *Wise Guys*. Warner Bros Pictures.

Melville, Herman. 1926. *Moby Dick*. New York: The Modern Library.

Messenger, Chris. 2002. *The Godfather in American Culture. How the Corleones Became "Our Gang."* Albany: SUNY P.

Puzo, Mario. 1969. *The Godfather*. New York: G. P. Putnam's Sons.

Reich, Jacqueline. 1993. "Godfathers, Goodfellas and Madonnas: A Pedagogical Approach to the Representation of Italian Americans in Recent American Cinema." *Voices in Italian Americana* 4.1: 45-64.

Renda, Francesco. 1978. *I fasci siciliani: 1892-94*. Torino: Einaudi.

Riis, Jacob. 1890. *How the Other Half Lives: Studies among the Tenements of New York*. New York: Charles Scribner's Sons.

Roberts, Sam. 2013. "Mario Cuomo, Vocal Foe of Italian Stereotyping, Finally Sees 'The Godfather'." *New York Times*, Oct. 21. https://www.nytimes.com/2013/10/22/nyregion/mario-cuomo-vocal-foe-of-italian-stereotyping-finally-sees-the-godfather.html?searchResultPosition=6.

Russo, John Paul. 2011. "The Hidden Godfather: Plenitude and Absence in Coppola's Trilogy." In *The Italian in Modernity*, by Robert Casillo and John Paul Russo, 434-492. Toronto: U of Toronto P.

Ruvoli, Joanne. 2018. "The Italian American Family and Transnational Circuits." In *The Routledge History of Italian Americans*, edited by William J. Connell and Stanislao Pugliese, 403-414. New York: Routledge.

Savatteri, Gaetano. 2017. *Non c'è più la Sicilia di una volta*. Bari: Laterza.

Schmalz, Jeffrey. 1985. "Cuomo Condemns Use of 'Mafia' for Describing Organized Crime." *New York Times*, Dec. 18. https://www.nytimes.com/1985/12/18/nyregion/cuomo-condemns-use-of-mafia-fordescribing-organized-crime.html.

Sollors, Werner. 1996. "Foreword: Theories of American Ethnicity." In *Theories of Ethnicity: A Classical Reader*, edited by Werner Sollors, x-xliv. New York: New York UP.

Tamburri, Anthony Julian. 2018. "Italian Americans and Television." In *The Routledge History of Italian Americans*, edited by William J. Connell and Stanislao Pugliese, 451-463. New York: Routledge.

Tolkin, Michael, Creator. 2022. *The Offer*. Paramount+.

Verga, Giovanni. 1925. "Liberty." In *Little Novels of Sicily*, trans. D. H. Lawrence, 197-209. New York: Thomas Seltzer.

"Fredo, I'm here on business…"

What *The Godfather* Did to Me, You, and the U.S.[1]

FRED L. GARDAPHE

WHAT *THE GODFATHER* DID TO ME

One day — a day of no special occasion — my Aunt Irene broke our family's book-as-gift taboo by giving my mother a copy of Mario Puzo's *The Godfather*; she told my mother that if her nephew was so intent on reading, he might as well read a book about Italians (neither of them had read it of course). The book's title was quite appropriate since, due to my father's early death, I, at the age of ten, had been made godfather to my cousin Michael.

The year was 1969. The novel lay unread until I found out that there was an excellent sex scene on page twenty-six. That's where I started reading. I sped through the book, hoping to find more scenes like the one in which Sonny seduces the maid-of-honor at his sister's wedding. Along the way I encountered men like Amerigo Bonasera, the undertaker, Luca Brasi, the street thug, and Johnny Fontaine, who were no different from the regulars who frequented my grandfather's pawnshop. Some would come in with guns, jewelry, and golf clubs to pawn. Men like these formed alliances to get things done — legally and illegally.

Because of its stock of familiar characters, *The Godfather* was the first novel with which I could completely identify. The only problem I had was that this thing the

---

[1] I have reprised pages and paragraphs from two earlier publications to weave this essay for this occasion. See especially, "Breaking and Entering," and *From Wiseguys to Wise Men*.

Re-Thinking The Godfather: *50 Years Later* (2024): 47-66

news media called *mafia* was unknown to me. Of course, I was familiar with the word *mafioso*, which I had often heard in reference to neighborhood troublemakers who dressed as though they were rich. That these guys could have belonged to a master crime organization called *Mafia*, was something I had never fathomed. The world that Puzo created, taught me how to read the world I was living in, not only the world of the streets, but the world within my family, for despite the emphasis on crime, Puzo's use of Italian sensibilities made me realize that literature could be made from my own experiences.

The novel came out after my grandfather was killed in a hold-up at the pawnshop. With him gone, the business was sold, and I was free to find my own way through the world. One of the ways I searched was crime. All throughout my high school years, I was accused of being in the *mafia* simply by being Italian and living in an enclave populated by some of Chicago's major crime figures. So, during my senior year, I decided to investigate the subject through my semester-long thesis paper that my Irish-Catholic prep school required. I decided it was time to find out what this thing called mafia was. This was the first writing project to excite me. The more research I did, the more I learned about the men I thought I had known. Whenever I saw familiar names, I would be amazed that they had done something so important that someone had taken the time to write about them. People never talked, in public at least, about these men.

One night I was in the back room of a restaurant for a private party given by my employers. I was the youngest employee, and as we were being served my boss turned the group's attention to me by proudly asking what I had been doing in school. I told them, quite loudly, that I was doing a research paper on the Mafia. When he asked what I was reading, I blurted out, *The Valachi Papers.* Everyone stopped talking and turned to me. I was shocked by the sudden silence; my eyes went around the table, and I realized that there were men in that room who had their names in that book. Someone changed the subject. and nobody said another word about my project.

When I completed the paper, I was certain of an excellent grade. The grading committee decided that the paper, although well written, depended too much on Italian sources, and because I was also Italian my writing never achieved the necessary objectivity that was essential to all serious scholarship. I read the "C" grade as punishment for my cultural transgression and decided to stay away from anything but English and American literature in my future formal studies.

I did, however, continue to search for and read books about organized crime. The way a convict becomes a better criminal by going to prison, I became an expert in the history of Italians in organized crime by reading. I would read the books and then tell the guys about what I had read. Kids would come up to me and ask what I had read about their fathers or uncles. I was christened with the nickname, *professore,* and many were the times when local gang leaders would use my stories to help them organize their activities. My knowledge of Roman history and Caesar's war stories, gained through my prep school studies, helped them create organizational structures that were as sophisticated as any the FBI could imagine.

I soon found myself taking in money without having to do much. Younger kids, anxious to be a part of our gang, took over the leg work at our direction. The older guys had their eyes on me, but when the Army draft became a threat, I disappointed them by going to college where I would find my way to more of Puzo's writing.

I soon learned that interpretations of the Italian American family take on new dimensions in Mario Puzo's novels. The image of the honest, hardworking Italian immigrant family portrayed in his earlier work is abandoned for the portrayal of the family able to gain the power through whatever means possible — legal or illegal--necessary to control their environment. This control is represented through the figure of the godfather, a figure which belongs to the second most important category in the hierarchy of Italian family order which Richard Gambino has described as consisting first of family members, followed by godparents — "a relationship that was by no means limited to those who were godparents in the Catholic religious rites...and which would better translate as 'intimate friends' and 'venerated elders' (*Blood* 20), then "*amici* or *amici di cappello* (friends to whom one tipped one's hat or said 'hello'), meaning those whose family status demanded respect, (*Blood* 21)" and finally *stranieri* (strangers), a designation for all others (*Blood* 21).

I began to realize that these levels of relationship serve as buffers designed to protect the family. With the nuclear family in the center, surrounded by the extended family, then by the *compari* and *commari,* (the men and women from their ancestral home) then *amici,* or non-related friends of the family, the order of the family works like walls around a castle. *Compareggio,* or godparent-hood, brings others into the family because a trust had been established between the two that is stronger than any other relationship an Italian can have. Traditionally, godparents would be chosen from the circle outside of the "blood" family for the purposes of cementing a family-like bond between those involved. Godparents would be selected based on their abilities to contribute to the protection and well-being of the family and selection of the most advantageous people was often a strategic, political decision for the parents.

In America, especially during the Depression era, those who held power in the Italian American communities (even gangsters) would be besieged with requests to be Godfathers or Godmothers to those who lacked access to power. It is not uncommon for a single individual to be godparent in dozens of families. In return for accepting the honor of being Godparent, the Godfather or Godmother's first name often became the second name of the child at Baptism or the third name of a child at Confirmation. The Godparent would be expected to assist the Godchild throughout life and act as a counselor and a mediator, especially during intra-family disputes. If a parent would die while the child was still a minor, the Godparent would take over the child's upbringing.

This then is the background of the serious and sacred relationship in Italian culture that would become distorted through some of the literary and media representations that captured America's attention during the 1970s.

While I never encountered any works by Italian Americans in my college literature courses, I pursued a quest to read more of his work and soon found out that *The Godfather* was the third novel written by Puzo. His earlier novels were his attempts to fulfill a dream of becoming an artist and escaping the ghetto world in which he had been born. Like John Fante, Pietro di Donato and Jerre Mangione, Puzo's early encounter with such writers as Dostoevsky in his local library strengthened his belief in art and, enabled him to "understand what was really happening to me and the people around me" ("Choosing a Dream," 24). It would not be art, but war that would enable Puzo to escape his environment "without guilt" (26). Out of his experiences in Europe during and after the Second World War he crafted his first novel, *The Dark Arena* (1955) and ten years later he returned to his life experiences growing up in a New York "Little Italy" to create *The Fortunate Pilgrim* (1965) which has become a classic of Italian American Literature.

In *The Dark Arena*, the protagonist, Walter Mosca (in Italian, *mosca* means fly) returns home from serving in the American occupation army in Germany. Unable to take up where he left off before the war, Mosca returns to Germany as a civilian employee of the occupation government and resumes his life as a black marketeer. While the novel received some good reviews, he was disappointed that it did not make much money ("The Making of *The Godfather*," 33). *The Fortunate Pilgrim* received similar notices and brought him even less of a financial reward. With such a poor earnings track record, no publisher would advance him the money he would need for a third novel. In debt to the tune of twenty-thousand dollars, he began to look for a way out. "I was forty-five years old," he writes, "and tired of being an artist" ("The Making" 34). Puzo draws on the experiences prior to writing *The Godfather* in creating the character Merlyn in his novel *Fools Die* (1978).[2]

With the publication of *The Godfather* in 1969, Mario Puzo was instantly promoted to celebrity status. Not since the publication of Pietro di Donato's *Christ in Concrete* (1939) had an American author of Italian descent been thrust into the national spotlight on such a grand scale. The timing of *The Godfather*'s publication had much to do with its rapid climb to number one and its long stay (sixty-seven weeks) on the *New York Times* best-seller list. The novel came off the press in the middle of the ethnic revival period of the 1960s. It also followed nationally televised Congressional hearings on organized crime and the publication of Peter Maas' non-fictional best seller, *The Valachi Papers* (1968), through which mobster-turned-informer Joe Valachi spilled his guts on his activities inside organized crime.

The Godfather has done more to create a national consciousness of the Italian/American experience than any work of fiction or non-fiction prior to or since its publication. It certainly was the first novel that Italian Americans, as a group, reacted to either positively or negatively. It appeared during a time when Italian Americans were just beginning to emerge as an identifiable cultural and political entity. Even though this book was much more a work of fiction than any of the earlier, more autobiographical, novels written by Italian Americans, the novel

---

[2] See especially pages 57-78 in *Fools Die.*

created an identity crisis for Italian Americans throughout the nation. Anti-defamation groups denounced Puzo for creating a bad image of Italians in America; young Italian American kids formed "Godfather" clubs; and real "mafiosi" claimed Puzo knew what he was writing about. For a while, Puzo wrote several essays about Italian America which appeared in major, national magazines. These essays, while often undermining the image of Italians that he created in *The Godfather* and his later novel *The Sicilian*, are also quite critical of the Italian Americans' criminal behavior in American society.

Since its publication, and especially since its film adaptations in the early 1970s, Italian American novelists have been writing in its shadow and until his death in 1999 Puzo, a recluse, took to writing screenplays for such films as *Superman* and *The Godfather Part III*, and two more novels, *Fools Die* and *The Fourth K* (1990). Though sociologists and literary scholars may forever debate the value of Puzo's work, it cannot be denied that he is one writer who has left a permanent imprint on the American cultural scene through his representation of *Italianità* and his creation of a mythic filter through which Italian American culture would be read.

WHAT *THE GODFATHER* DID TO YOU, THE ITALIAN AMERICANS

Prior to the event that prompted this publication, I had written extensively on the novel and its descendant films. I've reviewed the numerous occasions I have thought, spoken, and written about these, and what follows is a transcription of the presentation I made at the symposium.

Over the years, this novel has divided Italian Americans in terms of their responses to it. Just as Abraham Lincoln used a speech to unite a country at war with itself when he gave his address at Gettysburg that November 19 in 1863, my goal with the following section is to provide a way to situate this novel in terms of Italian America's quest for cultural integrity.

The Godfather Address:
An Icon's Impact on Italian American Culture

Two score and thirteen years ago, *The Godfather* brought forth on this continent, a new image of Italian America, conceived in one man's imagination and dedicated to the proposition that its author needed money to pay off gambling debts. Now we are gathered to examine the importance of this one book and the films derived from it, all of which instantly promoted a decent writer to national celebrity status. Not since the 1939 publication of Pietro DiDonato's *Christ in Concrete* had an American author of Italian descent been thrust into the national spotlight.

We have come to examine how this one novel has done more to create an intracultural struggle for identity than any work of fiction or nonfiction prior to or since its publication. But in a larger sense we cannot dedicate, we cannot consecrate, we cannot hallow this novel. The brave men and women, living and dead, who struggled with its pages have consecrated it, far above our academic power to add or detract.

The world might little note, nor long remember, what we say here, but it can never forget how this one work of art, the first that Italian Americans as a group identified with, changed how they were perceived, by others as well as themselves, right when they were just beginning to emerge as an identifiable cultural and political entity. Even though this book was much more a work of fiction than any of the earlier, more autobiographical, novels written by Italian Americans, it created an unprecedented identity crisis for Italian Americans by creating the illusion that behind every Italian American family, there could be a crime, causing great strife for those whose names ended in vowels as they tried to advance in their American lives.

It is for us the living, rather, to be dedicated here to the unfinished work which they who struggle here have thus far so nobly advance.

It is rather for us to be here dedicated to the great semiotic task remaining before us, that from this literary artifact we take increased devotion to that interpretative cause for which it served. We here should highly resolve that this novel shall not have been published in vain, that this community of Italian ancestry, shall have a new birth of freedom, and that identity of the people, by the people, for the people, shall not perish from the earth.

WHO'S AFRAID OF *THE GODFATHER*: READINGS AND MISREADINGS

The great electronic database in the cloud of culture we now call Google offers ten pages when you enter *The Godfather*, and 31,000,000 results. Compare that, if you will, to *Christ in Concrete*'s 99,900. Great Google offers nearly 2 million on the Puzo name alone. The number for other major writers of Italian ancestry don't come close, even when you add together: Pietro di Donato: 44,200;

Tina DeRosa 5,990; Diane di Prima: 109,000; Helen Barolini 13,400. This should give you a good idea of how large *The Godfather* 's shadow has been cast over Italian American culture.[3]

William Dal Cerro, in 1999, as Media Director of the Italic Institute, labored to count all the "mob movies" that came before and after: one hundred prior to the appearance of Coppola's *The Godfather*, and more than 300 made afterwards. And he judged that it was detrimental to Italian America's quest for assimilation.

No one took Puzo's novel seriously as a work of art, especially after the films made by Francis Ford Coppola. Art or artifice? Blasphemous or laudatory? Guilty or innocent? The debate over the novel's value that started then continues to this day, more than fifty years after the novel's birth. Tom Santopietro devoted a whole book to the examination of its legacy forty years after it appeared. He tried to explain the power that the films have had on group and personal identities: "For good and occasionally bad, in a manner comedic, serious, and oftentimes highly profound, *The Godfather* did nothing less than help Italianize the United States." However, just what is the Italianization that occurred is a question that Santopietro never answers.

Among the critics of Italian Americana, poet Daniela Gioseffi: "presentated [sic]" a talk fourteen years ago: crying that The Italian American mayor of New York "refused

---

[3] The novel even made it into "You know your [sic] Italian if...": the anonymous post that floated through cyberspace for years, at number 18. "Your favorite movies are: *The Godfather, Goodfellas, Bronx Tale, The Last Don* ... and you live by them."

to view or read *The Godfather*, as he feels a boycott of such works would serve us well, but one has never been fully instituted with political unity" (13). While Rudy Giuliani long proclaimed *The Godfather* his favorite movie and book." Gioseffi then went on a veritable rant.

> It was amazing to see that with all the good Italian American literature one could choose from, these professors, many Italians, spend time and funding analyzing fictional mob characters who are basically murderous, disgusting stereotypes. According to Camille Paglia, among many other cultural critics, these characters are poorly written soap opera types. Many realize that this decadent and degraded piece of pop culture has been hyped to a large degree in order to project all criminality on one ethnic group as a lightening [sic] rod to take attention away from the constant disclosures of larger, widespread cronyism on the part of corrupt governments...

Richard Gambino pointed to the psychological dangers this fiction brought forth in the land of Italian America.

> These false and toxic cultural mythologies form an important part of the matrix of influences which bear upon the formation of Italian Americans' personalities from before puberty, and the development of these through life to old age. The degree to which they affect any given individual varies, of course. It is hard to measure what any given individual's personality would have been, and how well it would have served him or

her, had these influences not been present. (It's a case of an historical hypothetical, e.g., like that of trying to know how American history would have been different if Abraham Lincoln had not been assassinated) ("The Curse")

Gambino offered his insights into why this act of one writer had such an effect on an entire U.S. American minority population.

The psychological benefits to many millions of individuals produces a great financial potential — people will buy what builds and reinforces the psychological benefits for them. Millions of people, as well as corporations, and institutions pay for films, TV shows, "journalistic" stories, books, etc. capitalizing (literally) on one or both two categories of slurs on Italian Americans. In fact, the public can't get enough. So, after *The Godfather* novel and films, we have *The Sopranos*. And "The Fonz" just opened up greater possibilities for *Jersey Shore*.

Gambino went on to explain just how this novel worked its charm to distort the very soul of Italian America.

But in the field of psychology there is a consensus regarding problems of personality. And part of the consensus is that confusion has deleterious effects on personality formation and development. The kind of confusion and distraction inflicted on Italian Americans from their childhood on by the virtual culture they are told is their reality versus their experienced personal cultural reality. The confusion born of experiencing two conflicting realities at once produces in Italian Americans behaviors associated with anxiety, doubt, shame, withdrawal, acting out, anger and rage, defiance, resignation, depression — all the classic "symptoms," if you will, of basic personality or identity confusion. (Again, which of these, or which mixtures of these, and the degrees of their virulence, differs from individual to individual.) But the results are also classic in clinical psychology: all of them result in an individual being self-distorting, self-limiting and self-defeating.

And so, despite what most critics of Italian America have written, many Italian Americans, especially those who belong to organizations, continue to be afraid of *The Godfather*, a fear that persists today, forcing somewhat educated people to transfer their very identities to once revered historical figures, such as Christopher Columbus, who through new research are revealed to other than what they once seemed. Yes, once upon a time there was a novel that so damaged the very people of which the author wrote, that even after the author died, the story continued to be written by others. Proving the Capitalist theory of criticism, that the successful book is the one that a film is made from that makes many millions of dollars. Could anything save this novel as a work of art?

WHAT THE GODFATHER DID TO THE U.S.

Against the tide of negative criticism, I proffer the possibility that Mario Puzo might have done Italian America a favor by creating a figure that can be read as a culture hero.

While the gangster has been an attractive figure in popular culture ever since his arrival on the silver screen in the early 1930s, it was not until Mario Puzo created Don Corleone that the figure began to achieve God-like status. One of the reasons for this is, as writer Robert Viscusi was so fond of saying, Don Corleone is the first fictional gangster who is not presented as a psychopath the way earlier ones lead Robert Warshow to write: "The quality of irrational brutality of rational enterprise become one. Since we do not see the rational and routine aspects of the gangster's behavior, the practice of brutality — the quality of unmixed criminality — becomes the totality of his career. At the same time, we are always conscious that the whole meaning of this career is a drive for success: the typical gangster film presents a steady upward progress followed by a very precipitate fall" (102). Puzo did not employ this tried-and-true formula for his novel, though as we know, Francis Ford Coppola employs it in the film versions through which he turns an Italian American story into an American morality play. When Vito Corleone commits a crime, we're right there with him and know the thinking that precedes the act and the emotional responses that follow. Vito Corleone is not a ruthless gangster who kills to simply defy authority, like Rico "Little Caesar" Bandello, or to advance his own career as Tony "Scarface" Camonte. Vito Corleone is not a dirty old man; he is "straightlaced about sex" (386), never so much as flirts, and exhibits only the most wholesome of behavior around women and men alike. At the end of the novel, Vito's son Michael does not have the fall, that Coppola will end up giving him in the second film. Puzo's humanized depiction of Don Vito has gone on to inspire dozens of imitations in subsequent novels and films and to influence artists and cultural critics alike to think differently of Italian culture in the United States. Among those critics is Camille Paglia, who in a 2002 forum presented by the National Italian American Foundation, held Puzo and Francis Coppola's versions of the Italian American gangster to be far superior to others, such as David Chase's creation of Tony Soprano, because of the way they depicted "the dignity of the Italian American male."

Reading the dons Corleone (Vito and his son Michael) as U.S. culture heroes, to my knowledge, has never been done, and perhaps this is because to do so would be to invite the wrath of the very culture that created this figure. Afterall, what could be so heroic about a gangster, the type of men my grandfather used to refer to as *lazzaroni* or lazy guys, because they made their money off hard-working people. But for a moment, I think it is important to consider the possibility of doing such a reading of this figure, for I believe that such consideration will reward us with better understanding of some of the fundamental issues developed in stories surrounding the American gangster figure.

Typically, culture heroes play a role in the creation and discovery of processes that enable a civilization to be born, saved, or to further develop. The very lives of culture heroes can describe how a culture has come to be and can also model behavior that is appropriate for civilized living. Often of divine birth, such as Isis of Egyptian culture Heracles of Greek culture, and sometimes a human whose actions preserve a culture under threat of extinction, such as Jesus of Hebrew culture or John Henry of African American culture, these culture heroes contribute something that fundamentally changes the way the affected cultures view the world. The gangster figure developed by Puzo functions in these and other ways. To envision the possibilities of divine birth for our gangster we need a little help from the late Robert Viscusi.

One of the aspects required of an Italian American culture hero is to show immigrants from his land how to use the best of Italian culture to survive in the new world. While assimilation to mainstream culture might be inevitable, if done on an immigrant's terms, it might be less traumatic and more rewarding, especially if that immigrant can profit from what he or she can use from the culture of origins. Thus, a key task for the Italian American culture hero is to defy total assimilation. In his essay, "Professions and Faiths: Critical Choices in the Italian American Novel," Viscusi introduces the idea that the Italian American novelist "brings to an American theme an orientation that is particularly Italian.... The American theme is professional life, and the Italian orientation grows out of the imaginative form that Christianity takes in the culture of the Southern Italian" (41). Viscusi identifies a suspicion that surfaces in the portrayals of working-class characters who enter professions and turn their backs on their ancestral communities. One example he uses to illustrate his point is a doctor in Guido D'Agostino's *Olives on the Apple Tree* (1940), who despises the immigrant culture so much that he strives to distance himself from it.

Beyond this idea of suspicion planted by these novelists, in terms of the consequences of assimilation and class mobility, Viscusi points to a more interesting notion in a later essay entitled "A Literature Considering Itself: The Allegory of Italian America" in which he introduces the idea that the "allegorical destiny of Italian American heroes, [is] to endure ritual death and processional re-identification in the process of becoming divinities" (272). It will be the children of these working-class martyrs who, learning the lessons of those who sacrificed their lives, become culture heroes of Italian America. We can see this through characters like Paul in *Christ in Concrete* by Pietro di Donato. In speaking about Italian American literature, Viscusi tells us, "It was clear to the discourse, if not to its explicators that no other role was open to Italians in the American imagination except that of divinities. The Puritans had preempted the role of moralists, [What R. W. B. Lewis called The American Adam] and the Blacks the place of the victim" (274-75). Like the life of Pietro di Donato's Geremio, Vito Corleone's life becomes a sacrifice that enables his children to realize better lives in the United States. But unlike Geremio, Vito's life becomes a model for his children to emulate, one that enables descendants to thrive in this new land.

So, what have we learned from seeing the gangster as a culture hero? In the end, while this novel has divided Italian America into those wannabes, those bes, and those who don't care at all, the time has come to ask the question, Who's afraid of *The Godfather*? Certainly not those

64

who have read the novel carefully. Perhaps only those who fail to see that as a work of art, *The Godfather* was, after all, only make believe.

WORKS CITED

Dal Cerro, William. 2023. "1914-2014: A Century of No Progress," at https://italic.org/wp-content/uploads/2021/04/filmStudySlides1228-1.pdf. Accessed 29 March.

Gambino, Richard. 1975. *Blood of My Blood.* New York: Anchor.

Gambino, Richard. "The Curse." http://sagharboronline.com/sagharborexpress/our-town/the-curse-of-italian-american-exceptionalism-12106

Gardaphe, Fred. 2006. *From Wiseguys to Wise Men: Masculinities and the Italian American Gangster.* New York: Routledge.

Gardaphe, Fred. 1995. "Breaking and Entering: An Italian American's Literary Odyssey." *Forkroads* (Fall): 5-14.

Gioseffi, Daniela. 2013. "Why Stereotyping of Italian Americans Persists: Imagining the New Italian American." *Pioneering Italian American Culture.* New York: Bordighera P.

Puzo, Mario. "Choosing a Dream: Italians in Hell's Kitchen". *The Godfather Papers and Other Confessions.* New York: Fawcett 1972. Reprinted in Thomas C. Wheeler. *The Immigrant Experience.* New York: Doubleday, 1971. Reprinted: https://www.latimes.com/archives/la-xpm-1999-jul-11-bk-54732-story.html. Accessed 28 March 2023.

Puzo, Mario. 1990. *The Fourth K.* New York: Ballantine Books.

Puzo, Mario. 1984. *The Sicilian.* New York: Ballantine Books.

Puzo, Mario. 1978. *Fools Die.* New York: Signet.

Puzo, Mario. 1972. "The Making of *The Godfather.*" *The Godfather Papers and Other Confessions.* New York: Fawcett.

Puzo, Mario. 1969. *The Godfather.* New York: New York: Fawcett.

Puzo, Mario. 1965. *The Fortunate Pilgrim.* New York: Atheneum.

Puzo, Mario. 1955. *Dark Arena.* New York: 1953. New York: Dell.

Santopietro, Tom. 2012. *The Godfather Effect: Changing Hollywood, America, and Me.* New York: St. Martin's P.

Viscusi, Robert. 1991. "A Literature Considering Itself: The Allegory of Italian America." Pp. 265-281. *From the Margin: Writings in Italian Americana.* Eds. Anthony Julian Tamburri, Paolo Giordano and Fred L. Gardaphé. West Lafayette, IN: Purdue UP.

Viscusi, Robert. 1983. "Professions and Faiths: Critical Choices in the Italian American Novel." Pp. 41-54. *Italian Americans in the Professions.* Proceedings of the XII Annual Conference of the American Italian Historical Association. Ed. Remigio U. Pane. Staten Island: American Italian Historical Association.

Warshow, Robert. 2001. "The Gangster as Tragic Hero," in his *The Immediate Experience: Movies, Comics, Theatre and Other Aspects of Popular Culture*, Cambridge, MA: Harvard UP.

"I never wanted this for you.... I thought that, that when it was your time, that you would be the one to hold the strings. Senator Corleone; Governor Corleone.... Well, it wasn't enough time, Michael. It wasn't enough time."

From "The Godfather" to "The Greedfather"
The Corleone Saga as Political Handbook

GEORGE DE STEFANO

Sun-tzu, *The Art of War*. Niccolò Machiavelli, *The Prince*. Antonio Gramsci, *The Modern Prince*. Mario Puzo, *The Godfather*. Written centuries apart, what do these works have in common?

Sun-Tzu's treatise on military strategy, which has influenced East Asian and Western philosophy and military thinking, focuses on alternatives to war — stratagem, espionage, making and keeping alliances, and the uses of deceit. Machiavelli's 16th-century political treatise, written to instruct royals in the art of governance, argues that the aims of princes can justify immoral means. Gramsci's work conceptualizes the modern prince as the disciplined revolutionary party, which he saw as essential to unleashing and mobilizing the creative energies of the oppressed.

As a novel and film trilogy, *The Godfather* is a saga of immigration and assimilation, a family tragedy, and, as Francis Coppola said, an allegory about capitalism and the American Dream. In the more than five decades since the first film's release in 1972, it remains enormously popular and influential, a popular culture phenomenon. *The Godfather* has influenced countless films and television series, including some not about organized crime, "Succession" and "The Crown" being two recent examples. But the Puzo-Coppola saga also exists as a template beyond the realm of art. Like the works of Sun-Tzu, Machiavelli, and

Gramsci, *The Godfather*, although fiction, is a political text often used to explicate strategies, tactics, policies, and personalities. In this paper, I discuss *The Godfather*'s continuing political relevance and how it is politically interpreted and instrumentalized. I cite U.S. and British political and media discourse; a book by U.S. foreign policy commentators that offers *The Godfather* as a guide to geopolitics in a post-911 world; and finally, I discuss it as a critique of capitalism, looking at the Mafia's business practices and their relationship to capitalism and politics.

Jonathan Freedland wrote in the British newspaper the *Guardian* that "anyone who has worked in politics will testify that the [Godfather] story is a set text for candidates, their advisers and those who watch them. It is revered for teaching timeless and universal lessons about power and authority, when to assert it and when to show restraint. Many is the fast-talking aide — whether in Westminster or Washington — who will identify a weak link in the campaign team or around the cabinet table as Fredo ... or an emerging threat who must be dealt with as Moe Greene" (Freedland, 2020).

Another *Guardian* contributor, Danny Leigh, wrote that former U.K. prime minister Boris Johnson "always names the climactic bloodbath of The Godfather as his favourite film scene ... a journalist reported him quoting the movie at a hapless photographer, Marlon Brando impersonation and all. Naturally, a joke is made of it. Still, the similarity with his style of government is obvious: a circle of cut-throats and suck-ups, rule by threat and favour. As ever, he echoes Donald Trump, whose whole shtick is Corleone cosplay" (Leigh 2022).

Long before the tousle-haired Johnson took up residence at 10 Downing Street, another conservative British prime minister, Margaret Thatcher, delivered a famous pronouncement that Don Corleone would approve. The "Iron Lady" declared that there was no such thing as society, "only individuals and families." The right-wing ideology of possessive individualism and loathing for progressive social policy (especially redistributive measures) finds its illicit analog in Cosa Nostra's amoral pursuit of its own interests in complete disregard for the effect of their activities on society as a whole. Thatcher, unlike Cosa Nostra, didn't murder socialist or communist activists and elected officials. But for many working-class, poor, and nonwhite Britons, and certain social minorities, her government's slashing of public services, including health, its attacks on organized labor, people of color, and gay and lesbian communities, produced a kind of social death. Thatcher's policies "were associated with substantial increases in socioeconomic and health inequalities" and the "unnecessary and unjust death of many British citizens together with a substantial and continuing burden of suffering and loss of well-being" (Scott-Samuel et al. 2014, 53, 66).

Thatcher's preference for privatized health care and aversion to publicly funded services remain a cornerstone of Tory ideology. The public sector is supposedly expensive and inefficient and needs to be replaced by free-market entrepreneurialism. Health and other public services should be delivered at minimum cost through contracts with low-balling private sector bidders. The Tories' ideological soulmates across the pond in the U.S. Republican Party also embrace privatization and the credo espoused by conservative activist Grover Norquist in 2001, who, sounding like a movie mobster, declared, "I don't want to abolish government. I simply want to reduce it to the size where I can drag it into the bathroom and drown it in the bathtub."

Italy's various mafias, with their well-known hostility to leftist politics (the roll call of communist and socialist politicians, union organizers, grassroots activists, and journalists murdered by them is depressingly long), share political conservatives' preference for privatized services. Cosa Nostra — as well as Neapolitan camorra groups and Calabria's 'Ndrangheta — invests in private health clinics, which are subsidized by lucrative government contracts. Such clinics offer services to reduce the workload for public hospitals, but contracts with these private entities have diverted funds from public hospitals in Italy, which are falling into disrepair. A two-tier health care system, with underfunded public institutions serving the poor and private facilities (albeit state-funded) serving affluent patients: a state of affairs greatly desired by right-wing governments and mafias. Mafiosi, however, have another reason besides profit to prefer private facilities: they are less likely to be recognized in them, and compliant administrators protect their privacy. Nonetheless, in January 2023, Matteo Messina Denaro, the Cosa Nostra chief who had been a fugitive for thirty years, was arrested in a privately-owned Palermo clinic where he had been receiving treatment.

∽

The Godfather, in its literary and cinematic incarnations, is a polysemous text that has been interpreted through different cultural and political lenses. Liberals and leftists appreciate the allegorical, Mafia-as-capitalism aspect; Barack Obama said the first film was his favorite movie. But far more often, the Puzo-Coppola epic has been a reference point for conservatives and their critics, including journalists who have used it to explicate right-wing politics. In the United States, two prominent right-wing public figures have exploited their *Godfather* fandom as part of their political personae: Donald Trump, with his "Corleone cosplay," and his flailing attorney, Rudy Giuliani. Trump has often spoken of his love of *The Godfather*, calling the first two films "classics." During his one-term presidency, the media likened Trump to a Mafia don so often that it became a journalistic cliché. The former New York mayor, who made his bones as a mob-busting prosecutor, liked to imitate Vito Corleone in public appearances. In 2001, at an annual event held by New York journalists, the then-mayor appeared as the cigar-chomping "Don Giuliani," accompanied by cast members from *The Sopranos.* He reprised this routine at the 2004 Gridiron Dinner in Washington. The Order Sons of Italy was not amused: "If Mr. Giuliani continued to do his Don Corleone imitation, that would offend and annoy a large number of Italian-Americans," a spokesperson said (CBS News 2007). Unperturbed by anti-defamation protests, Giuliani, at a 2015 campaign event, explained why reporters shouldn't write about his wife, Judy Nathan: "She's a civilian, to use the old Mafia distinction." In 2022, former Trump supporter and Giuliani fixer Lev Parnas took to Twitter to liken Giuliani's client Trump to the "Godfather" and said Giuliani was Trump's "consigliere." Parnas called Trump's White House Chief of Staff Mark Meadows "the underboss" and named the ex-president's "capos": Republican senators Lindsey Graham and Ron Johnson, Representative Jim Jordan, and Devin Nunes, CEO of Truth Social, Trump's social media platform (Teh 2022).

The ex-president and his critics have weaponized the name of the middle Corleone son, Fredo, as a term of disparagement. Trump delighted in taunting former CNN host Chris Cuomo by calling him "Fredo." But during his presidency, journalists debated who in his family qualified as a Fredo. A 2017 article in the online journal *The Conversation* titled "Who's who in the *Godfather* version of Trump's White House?" called Trump the don, "the head of the family in the same way that Marlon Brando's Vito Corleone was the head of his clan" (The Conversation 2017). As for his children, in 2016, Trump's eldest son, Donald Jr., met with a Russian lawyer to obtain damaging information about Hillary Clinton. In an attempt at pre-emptive damage control — the *New York Times* was about to publish the story — Trump's eldest son released a statement and screenshots of his incriminating e-mail exchange with the Russian on Twitter. Donald Jr's blunder, which only drew more attention to the *Times* scoop, elicited Fredo analogies from journalists, with *Vanity Fair* reporting that "it's no wonder that Trump's inner circle has been calling him Fredo since the campaign" (Desta 2017).

The ex-president's namesake, however, corresponds more closely to volatile Sonny Corleone, who responds to all threats with intimidation and violence. As his ill-considered tweet demonstrated, Donald Jr. is all too eager to "go to the mattresses" and wage a metaphorical war. Trump's second son, Eric, seems much more Fredo-like.

Eric was nominally in charge of Trump International Las Vegas; the Corleone family sent Fredo to Las Vegas to look after the Corleone casino holdings. "Poor Eric is rarely wheeled out to face the media," as the *Conversation* noted. "And he appears to embody many of Fredo's fictional flaws: he certainly doesn't come across as the sharpest knife in the drawer."

In *Vanity Fair* in July 2017, when the Trump administration was still "fresh hell," to borrow from Dorothy Parker, Yohana Desta argued that "Don Jr. is just the highest-ranking Fredo in an interchangeable lineup of Fredos. Why? Because each and every last one of the elder Trump children believes themselves to be the Michael Corleone of the family, which is the first rule of being a Fredo." Even Ivanka, who might seem the closest of the Trump progeny to Michael, was a Fredo because of her public gaffes, and so was her "nebbish" husband, Jared Kushner (Desta 2017). Speaking of Jared, the *New York Review of Books*' assessment of Kushner's memoir of his years as Trump's special advisor led with a *Godfather* reference. Like Don Corleone's youngest son, Kushner had a criminal father whose reputation and name he sought to rehabilitate. Reviewer Joshua Cohen noted that Kushner *pere*'s "yearning for legitimacy" recalled Vito Corleone's desire for Michael not to join the family business but instead enter politics. Cohen called Jared Kushner, the grandson of immigrants to New Jersey, "Don Corleone's dream come to waking life" (Cohen 2022).

The many Godfather-Trump comparisons notwithstanding, the ex-president resembles John Gotti more than Don Corleone. Most Mafia bosses were discreet and avoid-ed publicity, but Gotti craved the spotlight; all that media attention fed his ego. (Trump is, of course, largely a creation of the media.) In his book *People vs. Donald Trump*, former New York prosecutor Mark F. Pomerantz, who had investigated Trump's businesses, wrote: "He demanded absolute loyalty and would go after anyone who crossed him. He seemed always to stay one step ahead of the law. In my career as a lawyer, I had encountered only one other person who touched all these bases: John Gotti, the head of the Gambino organized crime family" (Rashbaum et al. 2023).

The trajectory from Don Vito to the Donald recalls Marx's famous remark about world-historic facts and personages occurring first as tragedy, again as farce. For one thing, the often-hysterical Trump has little of the fictional don's acumen, self-control, and discipline: he's all bluster and bullying. He evidently never learned Vito Corleone's lesson: "Keep your friends close, but your enemies closer." The Godfather's relationships were transactional, except for his family and trusted friends. Likewise with Trump, but the ex-president has few friends, and they become enemies the second they disagree with him, earning banishment and mockery in the media. Don Vito would never be so vulgar. Or so obvious.

Comparing Trump and his kin to the Corleones might be an amusing diversion. But as historian Russell Shorto wrote in 2021, the similarity between Trump and a Mafia boss is alarming and far from anomalous in U.S. history (Shorto 2021):

A wail of lament that echoed throughout Donald Trump's presidency was that he ran the country like a mob boss.

It wasn't just his having mentored with Roy Cohn, the infamous Mafia lawyer, or rubbed shoulders throughout his career with guys like Anthony "Fat Tony" Salerno. It was the wanton disdain for democracy, the venality and corruption, the aggressive pursuit of regulatory roll-backs, which did nothing for the economy, enriched a few fat cat friends and industries and degraded the quality of life for everyone else. It was the thuggishness of it all. So why was Trump adored by millions of Americans? Why, from his Mar-a-Lago hideout, is he still a threat? I think it's because the values he espoused — a rapacious free-market approach coupled with a screw-you crony-ism — are a mainstay of American history. Through some kink in our national psyche, gangsterism is seen by many as synonymous with American values.

Shorto continued:

The robber barons of old, the men who founded American capitalism in the industrial era, behaved exactly like mob bosses, plundering, bribing and pillaging their way to the top. John Jacob Astor got rich by swindling Native Americans and smuggling opium. Cornelius Vanderbilt made a fortune during the Civil War selling the Union army unseaworthy vessels. Leland Stanford advanced his Central Pacific Railroad by wantonly bribing Congressmen. Stock fraud, war profiteering, illegal monopolies: for all intents and purposes the men who built America were thugs. But they weren't imprisoned for crimes. They were lionized as visionary leaders, American icons.

75

This is where Coppola's conceptualization of the Mafia as a metaphor for capitalism and Trump as a crime boss converge: in the history of U.S. capitalism, from the robber barons to today's corporate chieftains.

Shorto's family name originally was Sciotto; his Sicilian forbears changed it when they immigrated to the United States. Researching the Sciottos' history, he discovered that his grandfather and father had been mobsters in southwestern Pennsylvania during the 1940s and 1950s. They were "consciously mimicking the establishment system to which they'd been denied access," Shorto observed. "Maybe the clearest indication of their hero worship was in aliases. The two alter-egos that my grandfather's partner used were Forbes and Ford."

Shorto noted that "the very term 'organized crime' came into being as a way to distinguish immigrant gangs from 'respectable' American practitioners of the same art form." "Many of our corporate leaders have behaved far worse than my grandfather. Until recently, though, they hid their excesses behind a veil of decency. Trump's accomplishment in office was to rip away the veil."

Corleone political analogies don't end with Trump, his family, or Rudy Giuliani. In an August 2022 letter to the editor, a *New York Times* reader wrote that South Carolina senator Lindsey Graham reminded him of Senator Pat Geary, a character in Godfather II. Recall the scene at Lake Tahoe when Geary contemptuously tells Michael that he intends to "squeeze" him for the gaming license Michael must acquire for the family's casino. Michael replies that not only will he not cough up any bribes, but the senator, not he, will pay the license fee. Soon afterward,

Geary is caught in a compromising situation involving a dead prostitute. Tom Hagen then offers the senator protection from scandal. From then on, Senator Geary is the family's loyal retainer. "Kowtowing to Trump may simply be the price Graham & Co. must pay to stay in power," the *Times* letter writer noted. "Still, there's the nagging question: what might the Don have on them?"

A letter to the editor in the *New York Daily News* (September 2022) similarly observed, "So it turns out that all the writers and historians of NYC crime had it wrong. There are not five criminal families, there are six! Add the name Trump to Gambino and Columbo, with the Orange Don as the Greedfather. His line to Vice President Mike Pence — 'I'm not going to be your friend anymore if you don't do what I ask' — could have come straight from Mario Puzo."

The media offered Godfather analogies to Republican politics and the party's internal squabbles even before Donald Trump. When Republican House Majority Leader Eric Cantor lost his primary race in 2014, *Politico* correspondent John J. Pitney Jr., in an article titled "How The Godfather Explains GOP Leadership Politics," compared the jockeying among House Republicans to replace Cantor to the leadership struggle in the New York Mafia after the death of Vito Corleone. "House majority whip Kevin McCarthy," Pitney observed, "must have been wondering which of his ambitious colleagues would be Barzini and which of his avowed allies might turn out to be Tessio" (Pitney 2014).

In a 2009 book titled, *The Godfather Doctrine: A Political Parable,* two U.S. foreign policy analysts, John C. Hulsman and A. Wess Mitchell, argued that after 911, the United States faced a choice similar to the one that confronted the Corleone family after the attempted assassination of Don Vito. The book, or rather, book-length essay, presents Vito Corleone as emblematic of Cold War America, whose global power and geopolitical dominance are declining, threatened by new enemies who play by unfamiliar rules. The don's inner circle corresponds to three leading schools of thought in American foreign policy. Hulsman and Mitchell liken one camp to "liberal institutionalists"; they are represented by consigliere Tom Hagen, whose approach "is the outgrowth of a legal-diplomatic worldview" similar to "the liberal institutionalism that dominates the foreign-policy outlook of today's Democratic Party" (Hulsman and Mitchell 2008). Hagen believed the Corleone family's main objective should be "to return as quickly as possible to the world as it existed before the attack" on Don Vito. He maintained that the old Mafia order still held and that the Corleones should negotiate with the other Mafia families. However, for the consigliere's diplomacy to succeed, "it must be conducted from a position of unparalleled strength, which the family no longer possesses. Tom has lost the luxury of always being the man at the table with the most leverage" (Hulsman and Mitchell 2008). Sonny Corleone, the eldest son, was akin to a neoconservative hawk, advocating a massive show of force to ensure his family's supremacy in the Mafia. His approach is based on "the strategically reckless notion that risk can be eliminated from life altogether through the relentless — and if necessary, preemptive — use of violence" (Hulsman and Mitchell 2008). But it is the strategy proposed by Michael, the don's youngest and least experienced son, that defeats the threat from rival Virgil Sollozzo and enables the Corleone family to confront the "multipolarity" of the Mafia. Only Michael, the realist, understood the changing scene, recognizing the need for flexible combinations of soft power — diplomacy and persuasion — and hard power (no explanation necessary) — to protect his family's interests in a dangerous and rapidly changing world. The authors of *The Godfather Doctrine* unequivocally endorse Michael Corleone as their preferred model of U.S. leadership in the twenty-first century (Hulsman and Mitchell 2009).

Rather than offer a model for geopolitical leadership, *The Godfather* illustrates the similarities between organized crime and the routine conduct of capitalist states, according to a 2022 article in the British journal *The Quietus* (Moore 2022). Sam Moore, the article's author, observed that "backroom bribery, shadowy deals made within the mist of smoke, money tainted by murder, compliance through violence and lies of strength and safety. The Mafia and the government are the same monster; the system keeps them both powerful and well fed, capital their king." Mafia culture may valorize family and the interdependence of family members, but the real raison d'etre is making money; capital is king.

In the first *Godfather* film, Corleone capo Sal Tessio remarks, "It was only business," shortly before being killed for betraying Michael Corleone. "Killing your brother-in-law is business," Moore wrote. "Cutting off a horse's head is business. It's the cold hard competition of capitalism in its purest form — the type America and its behemothic corporations had been spreading around the globe. It was never personal when a government was overthrown, or a small business was bankrupted, or labour value driven down. It was only business" (Moore 2022). Missing from Moore's otherwise astute comments is any recognition that the British Empire was no slouch when it came to global capitalist depredations.

The first two *Godfather* films explicate the continuity between family-controlled Mafia enterprise and corporate capitalism. They depict the clan or small association, known by the sociological term gemeinschaft, as superior to a large institutional collectivity, or gesellschaft. The Corleone business is a family venture, wholly owned and operated. It is ethnically homogeneous and closed to outsiders. It is its own world, a counterculture, an alternative social order in which ethnic solidarity is a means to resist corporate control and assimilation into American society. Don Corleone articulates the Mafia philosophy in the meeting of the heads of the "Five Families":

> As for our own deeds, we are not responsible to the .90 calibers, the pezzonovanti who take it upon themselves to decide what we shall do with our lives, who declare wars they wish us to fight in to protect what they own. Who is to say we should obey the laws they make for their own interest and to our hurt? And who are they then to meddle when we look after our own interests? "Sonna cosa nostra," Don Corleone said. "These are our own affairs. We will manage our world for ourselves because it is our world, cosa nostra. And so we have to stick together to guard against outside meddlers. Otherwise, they will put the ring in our nose as they have put the

ring in the nose of all the millions of Neapolitans and other Italians in this country. (Puzo 1978, 291)

The Mafia, or at least Don Corleone's piece of it, is a well-run concern that takes better care of its members than does legitimate society. In Puzo's novel, as World War II rages, "...the Don could take pride in his rule. His world was safe for those who had sworn loyalty to him; other men who believed in law and order were dying by the millions" (Puzo 1969, 222). Don Corleone is shocked and uncomprehending when members of his organiza-tion, and his son, Michael, volunteer to serve their coun-try, an abstraction the godfather can't understand. When told that one of the enlistees had said, "America has been good to me," the Don curtly replies, "I have been good to him" (Puzo 1978, 222).

But ultimately, the entity that had seemed like a her-metically sealed world, a secret society based on ethnic tradition, is revealed as another manifestation of the cap-italist business ethic. In the first two *Godfather* films, Don Corleone's archaic order, born in rural Sicily, gives way to the Italian American regime of his even more ruthless son Michael, who builds the family business into a national corporation. In Puzo's novel, Don Corleone anticipates this transformation, telling his assembled mob confreres, "We have to be cunning like the businesspeople, there's more money in it and it's better for our children and grandchil-dren" (Puzo 1978, 290).

The film's depiction of an old, traditional Mafia, as in-carnated in Don Vito Corleone, that was rule-bound and concerned mainly with protecting the economic interests of its members and their families, is a sentimental fiction. Although the Sicilian Mafia did evolve from its founding in the late nineteenth century, its *raison d'etre* always was the attainment of wealth, power, and territorial control. Jane Schneider and Peter Schneider are American social scientists who lived and conducted research in Sicily over several decades. They and other scholars had understood mafiosi as mediators, "well placed through networks of 'friends of friends' who brokered favors for businessmen, landowners, and politicians" (Schneider and Schneider 2011). But because of the testimony given in the 1980s by *pentiti*, Mafia turncoats, and the work of a new generation of Palermo-based researchers, they realized that the Mafia "was and had always been considerably more institution-alized, modern, commercially engaged, and entwined with national as well as regional powerholders, than we had previously imagined" (Schneider and Schneider 2011, 3).

Historically, rural mafiosi protected the holdings of small and large landowners, extorting from them the fee known as *pizzo* (beak-full). Many leftist intellectuals, who viewed the Mafia as "the product of an obsolete agrarian class structure," thought that the urbanization of Sicily after the Second World War would herald the Mafia's disappearance. However, "mafia bosses, capital, and methods penetrated the expansion of the urban environment, evident in patterns of rigged bidding, protection racketeering, and bribery in the construction industry." Leftist Sicilian intellectuals such as Mario Mineo began to write about an urban "borghesia mafiosa" (Schneider and Schneider 2011, 5).[1]

The view, expressed by researcher Pino Arlacchi and others, that a "traditional" rural Mafia had become a modern "enterprise Mafia" fell by the wayside. In his influential book *Mafia Business: The Mafia Ethic and the Spirit of Capitalism* (Verso 1986), Arlacchi, from Calabria, characterized that region's organized crime syndicate, La 'Ndrangheta, and Sicily's Cosa Nostra as "mafia," similar forms of territorial-based organized crime. He argued that the Sicilian Mafia was originally a form of behavior and a kind of power, not a formal organization (Arlacchi 1986, 4). In Sicily, the "traditional" rural Mafia was "separated from the Mafia of today" by a "great transformation" that occurred after the Second World War. In the 1950s and 1960s, the emigration of Sicilians to northern Italy and state intervention in the form of increased employment opportunities in non-agricultural economic sectors depleted the ranks of Sicilian males from which Cosa Nostra could recruit new members (Arlacchi 1986, 57). Jane and Peter Schneider, who lived in the western Sicilian town of Sambuca in the mid-1960s, similarly observed that "land reform, by mechanizing agriculture, had underwritten a massive exodus of rural labor" (Schneider and Schneider 2011, 5).

---

[1] When Matteo Messina Denaro was arrested in Palermo, where he had lived openly for thirty years, a prosecutor said that the fugitive Cosa Nostra boss had been helped by members of the *borghesia mafiosa*, local professionals, entrepreneurs, and politicians, who collaborated with Messina Denaro in various ways, including laundering his money.

According to Arlacchi, the 1970s — when he conducted his research — saw the emergence of an "entrepreneurial" Mafia whose members were better educated and less likely to come from the ranks of "lower classes" than the earlier, rural-based Mafia (Arlacchi 1986, 115). Mafiosi attained "autonomous entrepreneurial power" through their dominance of the international drug trade and other illegal domestic and international economic activity. They had easy access to Italian and foreign banks and attained "considerable political autonomy" through influencing election outcomes and mutually enriching relationships with compliant elected officials (Arlacchi 1986, xiv). Arlacchi argued that the seriousness of the Mafia phenomenon lay in its growth from "an unproductive, subordinate element in the economy" to "a productive force embedded in southern Italian socioeconomic structures" (Arlacchi 1986, 115). Previously, mafiosi invested earnings from their illicit businesses into those businesses, but the new entrepreneurs preferred to invest such earnings in legal businesses. But if the Mafia entrepreneurs were "productive," they were still predatory and parasitic. They took over businesses they invested in; used them for illegal purposes, such as money laundering; provided products and services of low quality, particularly evident in the construction industry; fought unions, and held down wages (Schneider and Schneider 2011, 5–6). They also continued to extort legitimate businesses for "protection" money.

As the Sicilian historian Salvatore Lupo convincingly showed, commercial engagements had been integral to the Mafia's development from the start, whether they involved sulfur mining, the export of citrus fruit to Europe and the

United States, the shipment of tobacco and morphine, or the sale of rustled animals and stolen meat. Moreover, Lupo's research demonstrated that the Sicilian Mafia had never confined its activities to the countryside but always had urban commercial interests, mainly in Palermo, the city and province (Lupo 1996, 9). Lupo was scathing about Arlacchi's Mafia historiography, and especially about his distinction between "the figure of the old mafioso. . .poor and in any case scornful of wealth, eager only to win social consideration" and "a modern entrepreneurial Mafia, a creation of the 1970s, eager to amass wealth and especially focused on drug trafficking, as ferocious as the previous Mafia was moderate." Arlacchi's "conceptual contrast" was "excessively clearly delineated" and "unpersuasive" (Lupo 1996, 13). Lupo's and other research reinforced the Schneiders' evolving view of the Mafia as "integral to capitalist development, even if its 'trademarked' means of production, the capacity of its members to exercise physical violence, contrasts with capitalists' general tendency to cede this capacity to the state" (Schneider J and P Schneider 2011, 16). The Sicilian Mafia was "a normal facet of capitalism," rooted in its political economy as much as capitalisms described as "merchant," "industrial," or "finance" (Schneider and Schneider 2011, 3).

Although Arlacchi's contention that the Sicilian Mafia originally was "a form of behavior and a kind of power" rather than a formal organization was inaccurate, the various *cosche* ("families") were not linked in a collectivity until the mid-twentieth century; rather, they were "a mosaic of small republics" operating within defined geographic territories (Gambetta 1996, 110-12). In the 1980s, Mafia "pentito" Tommaso Buscetta revealed to magistrate Giovanni Falcone that Cosa Nostra indeed was a structured, pyramidical organization with a "cupola" or commission at its apex. The Cosa Nostra leaders who comprised the cupola ruled on Mafia business activities and settled disputes. Buscetta also disclosed that the first Cosa Nostra commission was formed in 1958 after several meetings held the previous year in Palermo. Before the commission was established, senior members of the most powerful *cosche* met informally to coordinate their activities. The commission formalized these occasional meetings into a permanent body (Paoli 2003, 52–55).

But if the Sicilian Mafia is a structured, capitalist enterprise, how is it one? Mafia capitalism is both a violent and parasitic form that preys on legal business and organized illegality existing in a symbiotic relationship with legitimate business, politics, and the state. Sicily's Mafia employs a "twofold organizational model," one based on "protection/extortion," the other "more fluid and profiteering." These functions "interact, clash, and in any case tend to be linked together" (Lupo 1996, 18). Researcher Antonio De Bonis emphasizes the latter, noting that the Mafia "consistently penetrates the economy and government ... while preserving its own instruments of violence ... [it] cannot exist without the state and the capitalist economy, and it uses their resources in its own interests." De Bonis identifies four means by which the Sicilian Cosa Nostra and other Italian organized crime groups control economic activities: the issuing of concessions and administrative permits by the state; acquisition of contracts, utility agreements, and state orders; interfering in elections to promote candidates from Mafia organizations, which affects national government entities; and speculative investment of illegally obtained funds into financial and other commercial activities and real estate (De Bonis 2015).

In *The Godfather* and real life, the Mafia is a dual power with internal relations, rituals, and rules. But it is embedded in a political economy at the service of capital. Whether the corporate world is "worse" than the Mafia, as Russell Shorto argues, the two spheres are co-constitutive, even structurally inseparable. Returning to the forty-sixth U.S. president, Donald J. Trump, before he entered politics, did business in industries — development, casinos, and luxury real estate — that were "infested with organized crime" (Bruney 2020). Pulitzer Prize-winning journalist David Cay Johnston, writing at the time of Trump's first presidential run, observed that "no other candidate for the White House this year has anything close to Trump's record of repeated social and business dealings with mobsters, swindlers, and other crooks" (Cay Johnston 2016). According to the late investigative reporter Wayne Barrett, Trump went out of his way not to avoid contacts with the Mafia "but to increase them" (Bruney 2020). When the future president was building Trump Tower on Fifth Avenue in Manhattan, he hired the concrete company S&A, which was controlled by mobsters Anthony Salerno and Paul Castellano. Although most developers in the late 1970s and 1980s used steel to construct high-rise buildings, Trump chose to build with ready-mix concrete, whose production and sale were controlled by Salerno and Castellano. Because ready-mix concrete dries quickly, developers could experience costly worker slowdowns, a common tactic on Mafia-controlled construction sites. Trump bought Mafia concrete at artificially high prices, and, according to Cay Johnston, in exchange, he got labor peace, a "smoothly operating worksite" (Bruney, 2020).

Trump Tower was hardly the only instance of his business dealings with the Mafia. Trump bought the property for his Atlantic City casino from Salvatore Testa, a Philadelphia mobster whose father was that city's Mafia boss, Philip Testa. The casino was built by two construction companies controlled by notorious Philadelphia gangsters Nicodemo Scarfo and his nephew Phillip Leonetti (Frates 2015). Trump's connections to mafiosi continued in later years. In January 2023, the British newspaper the *Independent* published a 2022 photo of the ex-president posing with John Alite, a former hitman for the Gambino crime organization. Before the paper printed the photo with Alite, the *Philadelphia Inquirer* had reported that Trump had been photographed in 2022 with another gangster, Joseph Merlino, a Philadelphia Mafia boss during the 1990s, when Trump was operating his Atlantic City casino (Feinberg 2023). A Trump spokesman said the former president "takes countless photos with people. That does not mean he knows every single person he comes in contact with." The spokesperson did not respond when asked if Trump knew Merlino or was aware of his criminal background (Brennan 2023).

~

Francis Coppola has said capitalism was his central theme in *The Godfather*, and, in the fifty-plus years since the first film was released, both the Mafia and the economic system in which it flourished for decades have changed dramatically. In the United States today, and unlike in Italy, the Mafia is a husk of its former self, while capitalist dons, caporegimes, and their associates, working a corrupt, money-driven political system, get richer and more powerful. In the United States, economic inequality has reached grotesque levels; Republican policies, such as Trump's 2017 massive tax cut, have further enriched the party's core constituency, those whom George W. Bush gleefully called "the haves and have mores." In recent years, plutocrats Jeff Bezos, Elon Musk, Michael Bloomberg, and Carl Icahn paid no federal income tax (Eisinger et al. 2021). During the COVID pandemic, as millions lost their lives and livelihoods, billionaires' wealth rose more than $1.7 trillion, a more than 58 percent gain from 2020 to 2022 (Campo and Collins 2022). And there exists no social democratic party, much less a Gramscian revolutionary party, to mobilize and lead a popular uprising against the dictatorship of capital. Meanwhile, the United States as a polity frays and disunites, its deep contradictions of class (and culture) evidently unresolvable.

The Sicilian Cosa Nostra liked to pose as an "honored society" that protected the weak and defended Sicilian cultural traditions. Right-wing U.S. politicians similarly make populist claims when appealing to voters, declaring that they oppose liberal "elites" who want to impose socialism and "wokeness" on Americans. Many of them are multimillionaires who try to mask their commitment to increasing the upward distribution of wealth by posing as defenders of "religious liberty," "traditional" morality, and "freedom"; in reality, the freedom to act without any consideration of social consequences. However appealing to many, these ideological fictions cannot conceal that today, the Godfather's legacy is bequeathed not to an heir but to a class, the ultra-rich. Even more than the Corleones in their halcyon days, our world is "just business."

WORKS CITED

BOOKS

Arlacchi, Pino. 1986. *Mafia Business: The Mafia Ethic and the Spirit of Capitalism*, translated by Martin Ryle. Shocken Books.

Gramsci, Antonio.1959. *The Modern Prince and Other Writings*. New York: International Publishers.

Hulsman, John C. and A. Wess Mitchell. 2009. *The Godfather Doctrine: A Foreign Policy Parable*. Princeton UP.

Lupo, Salvatore. 2009. *History of the Mafia*, translated by Anthony Shugar. New York: Columbia UP.

Machiavelli, Niccolò. 2014. *The Prince*. CreateSpace Independent Publishing Platform.

Paoli, Letizia. 2003. *Mafia Brotherhoods: Organized Crime, Italian Style*. Oxford UP.

Puzo, Mario. 1978. *The Godfather*. Thirtieth anniversary edition. New York: Signet.

Sun-Tzu. *The Art of War*. 1994. New York: Basic Books.

JOURNALS/PERIODICALS

Scott-Samuel, A., Bambra, C., Collins, C., Hunter, D. J., McCartney, G. And Smith, K. 2014. "The Impact of Thatcherism on Health and Well-Being in Britain." *International Journal of Health Services* 44(1): 53, 66.

Schneider, Jane, and Peter Schneider. 3011. "The Mafia and Capitalism. An Emerging Paradigm." *Sociologica* Fascicolo 2, maggio-agosto: 1–22.

OTHER

Brennan, Chris. 2023. "Former President Donald Trump posed for picture with former Philly mob boss Joey Merlino at South Florida golf club." *Philadelphia Inquirer*, January 23.

Bruney, Gabrielle. 2020. "Netflix's Fear City Hints at Trump's Mob Connections. The Real Story Goes Even Deeper." *Esquire,* July 22.

Campo, Omar and Chuck Collins. 2022. "U.S. Billionaire Wealth Shot Up by $1.7 Trillion." *Common Dreams*, May 5.

CBS News. 2007. "Rudy's Love/Hate Relationship with The Mob." September 10.

Cohen, Joshua. 2022. "Lucky Guy." *New York Review of Books*, October 20.

The Conversation. 2017. "Who's who in the Godfather version of Trump's White House?" July 20.

De Bonis, Antonio. 2015. "Mafia: the State and the Capitalist Economy. Competition or Convergence." *Russia in Global Affairs*, November 12.

Desta, Yohana. 2017. "Is Donald Trump Jr. Really the Fredo of His Family? An Investigation." *Vanity Fair*, July 11.

Eisinger, Jesse, Jeff Ernsthausen and Paul Kiel. 2021. "The Secret IRS Files: Trove of Never-Before-Seen Records Reveal How the Wealthiest Avoid Income Tax." *ProPublica*, June 8.

Feinberg. Andrew. 2023. "New Trump photo with mobster surfaces a day after outrage over ex-mob boss photo op." *The Independent*, January 24.

Frates, Chris. 2015. "Donald Trump and the mob." CNN, July 31.

Freedland, Jonathan. 2020. "The Godfather: how the Mafia blockbuster became a political handbook." *Guardian*, October 31.

Hulsman, John C., and Mitchell, A. Wess. 2008. "A Foreign Policy You Can't Refuse." *Harper's Magazine*, July.

Johnston, David Cay. 2016. "Just What Were Donald Trump's Ties to the Mob? *Politico*, May 22.

Leigh, Danny. 2022. "This thing of ours: why does The Godfather still ring true 50 years on? From Succession to the real-life drama of the Tory government, the influence of Francis Ford Coppola's mafia." *Guardian*, March 4.

Moore, Sam. 2022. "The Most Powerful Man In America: The Godfather At 50." *The Quietus*, March 30,

Pitney, John J. 2014. "How The Godfather Explains GOP Leadership Politics." *Politico*, June 13.

Rashbaum, William K., Ben Protess and Jonah E. Bromwich. 2023. "Trump Likened to Mob Boss John Gotti in Ex-Prosecutor's New Book." *New York Times*, February 3.

Rosen, Kenneth. 2020. "The Mafia's Long-Shot Payout From a Medical Industry Takeover." *Newsweek*, June 13.

Scott-Samuel, A., Bambra, C., Collins, C., Hunter, D. J., McCartney, G. And Smith, K. 2014. "The Impact of Thatcherism on Health and Well-Being in Britain." *International Journal of Health Services* 44(1): 53, 66.

Shorto, Russell. 2021. "What My Mobster Grandfather Understood About American Capitalism." *Time*, March 17.

Teh, Cheryl. 2022. "Former Rudy Giuliani associate Lev Parnas outlined the branches of the 'Trump Crime Family' on Twitter." Yahoo! News. August 17.

Don Vito Corleone and Philip Tattaglia make peace as
Don Emilio Barzini applauds them.

Fredo greets Michael at Connie's wedding.

In Defense of Fredo

REBECCA BAUMAN

In the comedic mob film *Analyze This* (Ramis 1999), psychiatrist Ben Sobel (Billy Crystal) has become so preoccupied with his contentious relationship with a gangster patient Paul Vitti (Robert De Niro) that his own dreams become haunted by his newfound intimacy with the mafia. In a telling sequence, Sobel subconsciously reveals his own affinity with his patient's Oedipal complex when he has a nightmare in which he is the protagonist of an almost shot-for-shot reenactment of the attempted assassination of Don Corleone in *The Godfather* (Coppola 1972). Contrary to viewer expectations, however, it is the nebbish-y Sobel who is in the shoes of the august Don, whereas De Niro's Vitti takes on the role of Fredo, who memorably fumbles with his handgun at the pivotal moment in which the Don is shot and then crumples to the ground crying over his father's wounded body. When Sobel recounts his dream to Vitti, the mobster scoffs at its improbability: "*I* was Fredo? I don't think so."

The humor of this line comes not just from the viewer's extradiegetic knowledge of De Niro's long career in mafia movies and, more specifically, his own portrayal of the young Don Corleone in *The Godfather Part II* (Coppola 1974). Here, the character of Vitti affirms a common cultural understanding of the character of Fredo as the antithesis of the kind of masculinity that De Niro himself has embodied: ruthless, physically capable, cunning, and

Re-Thinking The Godfather: *50 Years Later* (2024): 95-122

resistant to all outward displays of weakness. The humorous line requires no explanation because it assumes a shared assessment of Fredo as a weak, ineffective character who violates the masculine norms that are intrinsic to the figure of the mafioso. Such cultural echoes as *Analyze This* patently demonstrate how Fredo's reputation has exceed his somewhat secondary status within the first two films of the *Godfather* trilogy, illustrating how he has become a watchword for a form of abject Italian American masculinity to be derided and scorned.

The films of course have established Fredo as a negative character through his betrayal of his brother Michael in *The Godfather II*, as Fredo violates the honor code in which all desires and allegiances extraneous to the mafia brotherhood must be sublimated else they be met with deadly punishment. Fredo's deviation from the honor code may be his death warrant, but it comes after the two *Godfather* films have already relegated him to an inferior position with respect to the family structure. The positioning of Fredo speaks volumes also about the longstanding family drama in Western culture and the trope of the less gifted child within the competitive dynamics of fraternal ascension. Fredo's significance as a character thus extends well beyond his transgression specifically within the hierarchy of the mafia family to express a more universal condition. It is logical then to read the widespread denunciation of Fredo as expressive of a commonly held anxiety, one that not only speaks directly to Italian American identity but to ideal masculinity in general.

All of this, however, risks overdetermining our understanding of Fredo both within and outside the diegesis of the trilogy. This contribution takes a closer look at the character of Fredo as he is constructed in the *Godfather* films, as well as in his afterlife in popular culture, in order to complicate the somewhat simplistic dismissal of Fredo for his negative symbolism. In his essay on *The Godfather* entitled "Michael Corleone's Tie," Anthony Tamburri encourages viewers to read Coppola's film semiotically, working through the film's "peripheral signs" as means of unraveling a more complex articulation of the film's preoccupations with such themes as good and evil (Tamburri, 70). My contribution here intends to do a similar reading via the character of Fredo. Indeed, it is through this character that we can see some of the more contradictory messaging in the trilogy and complicate many assumptions about Fredo's significance within the narrative. Fredo's inherent despicability, in other words, should not be taken for granted.

ANATOMY OF A FAILED MAN, PART I

While examining the representations of Fredo can reveal more nuanced understandings both of *The Godfather* films and of the shared anxieties revealed by his reception in popular culture, it is clear that Fredo is constructed as a failed man from the beginning of *The Godfather* trilogy. This is evident in *The Godfather*'s opening wedding sequence, much praised as a masterful piece of cinematic exegesis, which establishes the primary and secondary characters both by revealing their personalities while also signaling their future narrative importance. Although Don

Vito Corleone is immediately configured as the primary focal point, the future centrality of Michael is suggested by the repeated mentions of Michael's absence, building tension towards his eventual appearance that suggests his belatedness is a transitory lapse. Tom Hagen's presence as a rational commentator on events is demonstrated in his recurring interactions between the Don and the assorted guests who seek to meet with him. Sonny's outsized personality is revealed in various moments as he seduces and fornicates with a bridesmaid, quibbles with his wife, throws a tantrum at interloping FBI agents, and eventually submits to assisting his father in his ongoing business in his study. Connie's more circumscribed role, consonant with the portrayal of women within the films in general, is determined by her limited status as bride; and her mother's marginal status is also established in her solely ceremonial function as hostess of the event.

Yet amidst this visual exposition and the dialogue that serves to explicate the roles of each member of the Corleone nuclear family, the middle son Fredo is hardly mentioned. In fact, except for a wordless presence in the family photo ops, Fredo appears only in one short scene that appears to confirm his marginality both within the family and the film at large. As Michael and his date Kay sit eating and commenting on the variety of guests that surround them, an inebriated Fredo sidles up to their table, sits between them, and begins to paw at both of them in a way that appears to inspire both amusement and discomfort for Michael and Kay. While he wears the requisite tuxedo that most of the male members of the immediate family wear, his disheveled appearance and uncouth manners mark him as visibly unimpressive. With his lack of social graces or gravitas, Fredo clearly contrasts to the self-containment and sobriety of Don Vito, affirming that Fredo will not be seriously considered within the line of succession towards the Corleone throne.

In this sequence Fredo is already shown as deviating from masculine norms, which is apparent in his bachelor status. After all, this expository sequence affirms the heteronormative structure of the Corleone clan as they are each introduced in relation to their respective spouses or paramours. It is here that youngest son Michael's romantic commitment to Kay is officially proclaimed to the family; eldest son Sonny's machismo is affirmed through his extramarital coupling with his sister's bridesmaid; and even Tom Hagen has a brief interaction with his wife, whom is never again addressed in any of the films. Fredo, however, appears to have no date whatsoever, calling into question his heterosexual status. The family's awareness of his difference is suggested by the family photo posing that concludes the scene, with Fredo placed off to the side of the group where he stands behind Tom Hagen's children, both accentuating his childless status while also relegating him to an infantile position within the family.

The notion that Fredo is characterized by a lack is revealed not just by his solitude in scenes such as this, but also through his physical absence at pivotal moments. Throughout the film Fredo is missing from most scenes of family gatherings, particularly the strictly homosocial conferences that are concerned with family business. While he is seated at the Don's meeting with Virgil Sollozzo in his office, Fredo does not comment on the proceedings, nor is he present in the strategizing session that takes place beforehand. Puzo's book explains Fredo's removal from the family business in its initial description of his character: "[H]e did not have that personal magnetism, that animal force, so necessary for a leader of men, and he too was not expected to inherit the family business" (Puzo, 17). This becomes even more apparent in Coppola's film, where the possibility that Fredo might be aligned with his father's power is never entertained.

Indeed, the entire structure of *The Godfather* seems to affirm this by only showing one scene in which Fredo and his father speak to each other; significantly, this is the scene in which Fredo fails to ward off his father's would-be assassins. The attempted assassination scene is also a telling moment. The film faithfully follows the book as it describes Fredo, who has not reached for his gun in time to ward off the attack, so overcome with shock and despair that he falls to the ground in tears. In the film, after Fredo crumples to the curb the shot is framed so that we see only his legs and a pistol hanging limply in his hand; a deflated phallic symbol that suggests that Fredo's inability to swiftly react to his father's attackers is evidence that he is not a real man. As a close-up shows Fredo rocking back and forth weeping, he becomes definitively associated with the emotional realm, feminizing him further and forming a direct contrast to his brother Michael's more cool-headed response to the news of his father's wounding in the subsequent scene.

While his father's assassination attempt is pivotal in marking Michael's inevitable transition from law-abiding outsider into the family business, this also marks the further removal of Fredo from the inner circle of the Corleone organization. After this event Fredo is not included in any of the discussions in which his brothers organize their plans for revenge, presumably because Fredo is still emotionally traumatized by witnessing the attempted murder. In Puzo's novel, it is Sonny who specifies to Michael that Fredo has no place in the discussions: "Freddie is no use to us...He wasn't like you and me, Mike" (Puzo, 97). In the film, the lack of explanation over his absence reinforces the audience's perception of Fredo's negligible status precisely because his brothers don't seem to mention him at all. Even the adopted son Tom Hagen, who is de facto unable to take the position of Don due to his ethnicity and lack of blood ties, is more central to the family unit at these times. During one scene in the immediate aftermath of the shooting, when Tom suggests they make peace with Sollozzo in the event of Don Vito's death, Sonny calls into question Tom's loyalty, noting, "That's easy for you to say, Tom, he's not your father." Tom quickly retorts, "I was as much a son to him as you or Mike," completely eliminating Fredo from the filial hierarchy.

It is when his younger brother officially takes the reins of power later in the film that Fredo's failures are more pointedly denounced. In contrast to his previously scenes in which Fredo is usually a silent spectator to the family drama, once he is ensconced in the family-backed casino in Las Vegas he transforms into a more overt symbol of masculine inefficacy. Fredo is re-introduced as a flamboyant playboy, and as Puzo describes him, when Michael meets Fredo in Las Vegas he is "more dandified," dressed in an "exquisitely tailored gray silk suit and accessories to match" (Puzo, 383). In Coppola's film Fredo is more garishly attired in a yellow, wide-lapelled blazer that he wears over a black, point-collared shirt with matching silk scarf, beige checked trousers, and white patent-leather shoes. His ostentatious dress is nothing like his subdued and non-descript attire in his earlier scenes in the film, and indeed in style is more reminiscent of the 1970s disco fashions contemporaneous to the film's production. His immersion into the hedonistic atmosphere of Las Vegas is also suggested by the gold-rimmed aviator sunglasses that he wears even within the dim interior of the casino. Fredo's inability to read social cues or prioritize serious matters of business is evident as he surprises Michael with a party featuring a group of showgirls and a band playing "For He's a Jolly Good Fellow," to which Michael responds with obvious distaste.

While Fredo's exuberance and apparent ease with the Las Vegas high life suggests he is coming into his own, it provides another arena for displaying his failure to conform to the requirements of leadership, which is instead exemplified by Michael's disinterest in pleasure and his taciturn, almost lifeless demeanor. As Michael gains power, he increasingly becomes desexualized, a contrast to Fredo's newfound promiscuity in Las Vegas, which is also present in Puzo's original novel. Yet Fredo's heterosexual activities are not only ill-advised but also in direct conflict with the family's economic interests, for as Moe Greene complains, he has been jeopardizing business by "banging cocktail waitresses, two at a time." This unrestrained and inappropriate form of extra-marital coupling contrasts to the procreative activities of his brothers and suggests Fredo's inability to form proper attachments to women. Fredo's exaggerated pursuit of flashy women, in fact, suggests a compensation for his potential insecurity with his own heterosexuality.

Fredo thus lacks all the dimensions of both business acumen and masculine bravado that are prerequisites to acceding to mafia power. Yet there may even be something more damaged within him, which is suggested in the only scene in which Don Vito references his middle son. When the ailing Don has a heart-to-heart with Michael and reveals to him his dashed hopes that Michael could ascend to the highest ranks of legitimate American power, he tellingly does so by comparing Michael to his less-promising brothers: "I knew that Santino was gonna have to go through all this... and Fredo, well. Fredo was... but I never wanted this for you." This potentially damning denunciation trails off into an ellipsis that tantalizingly suggests that the Don can offer an explicit explanation of Fredo's failings. However, Don Vito's thought process is never revealed, leaving the spectator to conjecture what exactly Fredo *was* that earned him such dismissal.

ANATOMY OF A FAILED MAN, PART II

While Fredo is both increasingly disparaged and dismissed within the narrative of the first *Godfather* film, it is in *The Godfather Part II* that his shortcomings become central to the narrative and are deeply intertwined with the tale of Michael's character development into a ruthless and cold-hearted ruler. The climax of Fredo's story occurs with his betrayal of Michael, which occurs when he provides information or assistance to Michael's rival Hyman Roth that leads to an attempted assassination, in an echo of the similar attack on Don Vito in the first *God-father* film. While the extent of Fredo's role is left unclear, it is an action that definitively determines the transition of Fredo from not just a pitiable disappointment to the Corleone name, but indeed as perhaps the most offensive of all the characters in the trilogy.

As many studies of the sequel attest, *The Godfather Part II* relies on a series of parallels and inversions of motifs from the first film to demonstrate both the increasing power and downward moral spiral of its main character Michael. The expository opening sequence of a large party celebrating the confirmation of Anthony Corleone, Michael and Kay's son, serves the same purpose of the wedding sequence in *The Godfather* by establishing the current positions of the major characters while familiarizing audiences with new characters. In its depiction of the family celebrating in its new compound on the shores of Lake Tahoe, this scene illustrates the increased wealth and social prestige of the Corleone clan, which is accompanied by a loss of ethnic tradition and a marked estrangement amongst the family members. It is also in this sequence that Fredo's extremely precarious status within the family is even more pronounced.

When we first see Fredo amongst the guests as the large, outdoor reception, he is now dressed in a brown and black plaid silk jacket, a signal that his sartorial habits have become more moderate while still setting him apart from the more sober stylings of the other guests. Of all the family members, he appears to be the only one who is genuinely pleased to see Pentangeli, a member of Clemenza's crew who represents one of the last remnants of Don Vito's reign over the Corleone empire. Fredo, however, is again oblivious to the protocol that prioritizes serious business dealings when he expresses perplexity of why Pentangeli is not granted an immediate audience with Michael, who is occupied with more grave business negotiations with Senator Geary and Hyman Roth's emissary Johnny Ola. Fredo's naïve attachment to the old ways is reflected in how he toasts with traditional Italian phrase *"Cent'anni,"* an expression he finds he must explain to his clueless WASP wife, Deanna. Fredo thus appears as someone who has not effectively transitioned to the family's new status and is still awkward in its public face.

It is through the introduction of his wife, in fact, that Fredo's dubious sexual status becomes even more fully explicit. An attractive but flirtatious alcoholic, the blonde Deanna clearly in not integrated into the family fold. This is expressed first through her lack of familiarity with the family's cultural heritage and then in her eventual defamation of Italians, when she drunkenly proclaims, "Never marry a Wop, they treat their wives like shit." Fredo's attempt at marriage is further testament to his inability to properly embody the role of the dominant male, as he is unable to control his wife when she is falling down on the dance floor at the elaborate banquet. As Fredo attempts to disentangle Deanna from a man with whom she is dancing too intimately, she loudly berates him and reproaches him for his sexual inadequacy, "You're just jealous because he's a real man." Not only does this comment imply Fredo's sexual impotency, but she also speaks directly to assumptions about Italian American masculine supremacy connected to violence and control, when she shows herself to be physically unafraid of him and laughs, "You couldn't beat your mamma."

Fredo's unhappy spouse is a cautionary tale of how the degeneration of the Corleones arises when they stray from an ethnically appropriate union. Of course, by *The Godfather II* all the Corleone siblings have eschewed Italian American matches, shown in Michael and his mother's consternation at Connie's engagement to a blond gold-digger named Merle (Troy Donahue). While Michael too has deviated from the family bloodline by marrying outside the ethnic confines, his union reflects a far-sighted strategic positioning of the Corleones to be more visibly integrated with the status quo, so that even if its operations remain illegitimate it can mask itself more seamlessly within the dominant culture. Moreover, unlike his siblings, Fredo's marriage has generated no progeny, indicating another failure to fulfil one of the essential dictates of the Roman Catholic family union.

Fredo's haplessness becomes more sinister in the central section of the *The Godfather II* when his deceit to Michael is revealed. The suspicion that Fredo is involved has already been suggested in a scene between Michael and Tom Hagen, in which Tom questions why Michael is no longer able to trust his brother. Michael responds, "Fredo? Well, he's got a good heart. But he's weak and he's stupid, and this is life and death." The scene that follows this conversation shows Fredo in his marital bed, his wife asleep and turned away from him, when he receives a phone call that confirms his involvement in the conspiracy. The set design visually degrades the character by depicting him lying on black silk sheets, associating him with the lurid while also giving a dark, infernal atmosphere to his domestic realm. When we next see Fredo he is arriving at a hotel in Havana to deliver a suitcase containing two million dollars to Michael, and he comically struggles with a bellhop who attempts to carry the luggage for him. Fredo's incompetence is reiterated in a subsequent scene in which the two brothers share a drink at an outdoor café in the city. Fredo's dependence on alcohol is even more apparent, and his choice of drink is an effete banana daiquiri, which he is unclear on how to order in Spanish despite the revelation that he is a repeat visitor to Havana. Yet while this series of scenes demonstrates that Fredo is increasingly debased and unravelling, the dialogue opens a space for Fredo to voice his helplessness and despair over his situation. In his conversation with Michael, the despondent Fredo displays frustration with his inability to measure up to his family legacy, as he ruefully wishes he had married and had children, so "for once in my life I'd be more like … Pop."

Fredo's sense of his own failings is clearly reflected not just in the light of his younger brother Michael's prominent role in the family, but in his inability to emulate the standard established by the still-powerful memory of his father. Accordingly, Fredo is frequently associated with the matriarchal rather than with the patriarchal sphere of the family, and his wife Deanna's comment about his lack of physical menace and the reference to "your mamma" reminds us that Fredo is perceived as a mamma's boy. After all, Michael commands Al Neri that his brother's assassination be deferred until after the death of their mother, whose suffering would presumably be immeasurable with the loss of her middle son. This pairing of Fredo with the maternal is elevated to the religious dimension when Fredo is shown as a devotee of the Virgin Mary. This is revealed towards the end of the film after Fredo has been temporarily granted re-admittance to the family compound, when he explains to his nephew Anthony that, as a child, he always caught a fish because he had a special trick of reciting a Hail Mary whenever he dropped his line in the water. This poignant vignette, taken from Coppola's own personal history, displays Fredo as nostalgic for his one long-lost moment of superiority, and notably it is one that is indebted to the Catholic tradition of mother-worship. It is fitting then that Fredo is in the midst of reciting the Hail Mary at the moment of his killing; still earnest in the possibility that his salvation may lie in a gynocentric moral order that is ultimately powerless to the patriarchal logic of retribution represented by Corleone power.

RE-READING THE FREDO NARRATIVE:
AFFECT AND ANTICAPITALISM

While the first two *Godfather* films establish the figure of Fredo as decidedly abject, in reviewing the more minor scenes within the film one finds clues that linger on Fredo's subjectivity and suggest that in his repeated and prolonged denigration lies the film's greatest denunciation of the criminal logic that rules the Corleone family. The film's indictment of these values comes to the fore with Michael's downfall, but they are already present in the characterization of Vito Corleone in the first film. In fact, even as the films portray the Don as benevolent and motivated by values of justice and respect, Vito's paternal failings are the root of Fredo's fallibility, for Vito rigorously adheres to a paradigm for manhood that is predicated on the capitalist logic of economic preservation that prioritizes the family business interests above all. This is apparent in the way the family structure sidelines Fredo without attempts at inclusion. A notable example is the scene in *The Godfather* when the wounded Don finally returns home from the hospital to recuperate, and we see clusters of family members awaiting his arrival and lining up to greet him in his sick room. In every shot Fredo is placed on the far lefthand side of the screen, just as he had been in the initial wedding sequence, a form of demotion via the *mise-en-scene* that contrasts with the ways that Sonny and Michael are granted greater narrative prominence and agency by their positioning in the righthand side of the frame. As the assorted parents and children file in and lay upon the Don handmade get-well cards, we do not even see Fredo in this entourage. Instead, he appears briefly in one moment when Sonny announces to his bedridden father that Fredo will be sent to Las Vegas "to rest" and to learn the casino business. Fredo's future then is clearly the concern of his older brother and not one of his own choosing; moreover, this dialogue now gives us an indication that Fredo has suffered an emotional breakdown as the result of witnessing his father's attempted murder.

Following this scene, the family sits down to Sunday supper. The sequence is worth mentioning mostly because of a brief scene that immediately follows. Mamma Corleone sits at one end of the table with her back to us, in keeping with her role as the silent matriarchal anchor of the family, while Sonny as the interim Don is seated at the head of the table. Fredo again is seated to the far left of the frame and is silent as Carlo, Connie, and Sonny, occupying the middle of the frame, bicker about both family business and table etiquette. This contentious dinner scene then cuts to a shot of Fredo, alone, silently entering the sickroom of the Don. Hands in his pockets and his eyes riveted on his father's bed, the camera follows Fredo as he crosses the room to a window seat and sits down without taking his eyes off his father. The next shot shows a medium shot of the troubled face of Don Vito, lying with his grandchildren's cards still sprawled across his chest as he stares off into the distance in the opposite direction of his middle son. This scene slowly fades from the Don's face to a shot of the Sicilian countryside, which is the first shot of the extended sequence the follows Michael's exile in his ancestral homeland. This overlay, which fuses the face of the Godfather with image of Michael strolling in the Sicilian landscape, suggests that all the Don's thoughts are focused on his favored younger son, and that he is either willfully or unintentionally oblivious to the presence of his middle child who is silently sitting in his room holding vigil.

While this brief sequence does hold a narrative function in providing a transition to the Michael-in-Sicily sequence, the presence of Fredo is not required in order to make this move from the Don's thoughts to his son's exile, prompting questions about what motivated the insertion of this scene. The scene is also remarkable because it is a rare moment in the film that places Fredo at the center of the frame. This is the first of the instances in both *Godfather* and *Godfather II* that offer insight into Fredo's state of mind and contextualize his personality and behaviors within a familial system that consistently refuses to consider his agency or listen to his perspective. In *The Godfather II* Fredo is finally able to give voice to his own sense of inadequacy and of being deliberately wronged within the ordered structure of Corleone succession. This comes to the fore in the confrontation scene with Michael after Fredo has been re-admitted into the family sphere at Connie's behest. Here Fredo explicates his decision to betray Michael, which stems directly from his systematic exclusion from meaningful work and a lack of recognition of his own abilities and talents: "Send Fredo off to do this. Send Fredo off to do that. Let Fredo take care of some Mickey Mouse night club somewhere. I can handle things! I'm smart! Not like everybody says!" This singular moment in which Fredo articulates his rage at his persistent devaluation is partially undercut by the staging, as Fredo is reclined in a lounge chair that places him well below Michael, who stands above him.[1] Fredo's weak posture in this scene also expresses a resignation to his inevitable fate; the death sentence that had been sealed with Michael's kiss in Havana and set in motion by an exchange of glances between Michael and his henchman Neri at Mamma Corleone's funeral that confirmed the order for Fredo's murder.

---

[1] This strategy that also ensures that the taller actor John Cazale would not tower over the short-statured Al Pacino.

Coppola was explicit about how he wanted *The God-father II* to communicate his own sympathies for Fredo, whose position the director locates in the cultural dynamics of the Italian American family:

> In an Italian family, or at least in my family, there are always those brothers who are considered not as talented as the others, that are made fun of. Maybe I was in that category some of the time, I don't know, I certainly had uncles that were put down. I think that Italians who come from that little town mentality are very hard on their own and very cruel to those who don't quite cut the mustard at the same level that the star brothers or the star uncles do, and I empathized a little bit with Fredo because he bungled guarding his father, the gun just totally slipped out of his hand in a very inept way, and I always thought of him and how he'd feel about it. He loved his father no less than the other brothers, and he must feel so responsible for what happened. I think maybe one of the good things that I was able to do was to have that perspective off the central action, which was of course the men doing men's business.[2]

Tellingly Coppola points to both the gendered and the economic thrust of those primary scenes and how they contrast to the spectacle of Fredo's drama, reaffirming that Fredo's internal tragedy resides outside the narrative concerns of masculine enterprise. Moreover, Coppola's statement emphasizes the division between the

---

[2] Coppola, DVD commentary to *The Godfather* DVD.

labor of affect versus the labor of capitalist enterprise, which affirms a reading of Fredo as symbolic of a rupture in the imperative towards the accumulation of wealth that motivates the majority of the action in the *Godfather* trilogy.

This reading resonates with a scene that occurs right before the conclusion of *Godfather II*, when a solitary Michael indulges in the memory of a pivotal moment in his youth. In this brief flashback we see the Corleone siblings gather to celebrate their father's birthday, which happened to coincide with the bombing of Pearl Harbor that signaled the entrance of the United States into World War II. As they prepare a surprise fête for the absent Vito, Michael announces that he has just enlisted in the Marines. Sonny responds with anger, chastising Michael for risking his life for the greater good rather than confining his primary allegiance to his family, a sentiment that all the siblings agree is consonant with the perspective of the Don himself. Yet despite the felt presence of Vito's disapproval, Fredo attempts to shake Michael's hand and tells him, "That's swell Mike, congratulations" before being violently hit by Sonny. As Fredo is sent out of the room by his domineering older brother, offscreen we hear that the Don has finally arrived, and the group abandons Michael to remain alone at the table while we hear the strains of the celebrants singing, "For He's a Jolly Good Fellow."

This is the moment in which Michael declares his attempt to depart from the hereditary code that places the family and its business interests above all other moral, ethical, intellectual, and emotional concerns. It is also revealed through a flashback that, significantly, comes right on the heels of the murder of Fredo that Michael himself has ordered and witnessed. That Fredo alone approves of Michael's defiant choice to fight in the war reiterates the notion that he and Michael, however briefly, had the potential to envision an existence independent of the totalizing view of the family and its business motives. The song heard offscreen celebrating the beloved father now takes on an ironic tone, as well as sonically creating a connection to the original *Godfather* film when Fredo had the band play the song upon Don Michael's arrival in Las Vegas. By creating these parallels between these two Dons, who are neither jolly nor good, Fredo becomes the link that unites these two criminal figures. The tragedies thus are double in the *Godfather* films: the moral downfall of Michael, who once demonstrated the potential to rebel against his dynastic inheritance, and the lifelong devaluation of Fredo, whose potential was never revealed.

FREDO'S AFTERLIFE

In 2012 a group of scholars published a paper in the *Journal of Business Ethics* in which they coined a new term, the "Fredo effect" (Kidwell, Kellermanns, and Eddleston 2012). According to the authors, the "Fredo effect" was defined by having a less-than-skilled member of the family in a significant position within a family business. The authors spoke sympathetically about the struggles of leaders of family firms who might be "reminded of Fredo as they gaze across the table at a holiday dinner and see a son, brother, daughter, sister, or other relative who—well intended or not—has proven detrimental to the family business" (Kidwell, Eddleston, Cater, and Keller-manns, 5). Within the schema outlined by these scholars, and in follow-up papers in which they further elaborate the dangers of having a 'Fredo' in the family business, they affirm what appears to be the legacy of *The Godfather* films, which is that families are threatened by weakness as it poses a danger to their well-being and, more importantly, to their economic interests.

While it is clear from such studies that Fredo is a recognizable shorthand for failure in popular culture, what is unique about the Fredo figure is that because he is integrated into the narrative of the mafia family, he has developed into an ethnically specific symbol both of abject Italianness and fraternal inferiority. This became abundantly evident in the 2019 news scandal when CNN newscaster Chris Cuomo exploded in rage after being called 'Fredo' at a public event [for a more extended discussion of this see George De Stefano's contribution to this volume]. Cuomo's explication that the term 'Fredo' was akin to the "n-word" aroused debate about Cuomo's drawing racialized equivalencies between terms with vastly different histories and cultural weight. Cuomo was supported, however, by a CNN spokesperson who supported Cuomo's reaction to being labeled with an "ethnic slur."[3] What was suggested, then, is that the very existence of Fredo is an affront to all Italian Americans.

What tends to get lost in the discussion of Cuomo's outsized response to the word, in which he threatened violence to the man who dubbed him 'Fredo,' are the

---

[3] Cf. Flynn.

personal insinuations that may have cut Cuomo to the quick. Would Cuomo have been so easily perturbed if he were not the younger brother of Andrew Cuomo, then-governor of New York state, a man who appeared to have ably stepped into the shoes of his illustrious father Mario and was aspiring to the highest office in the nation, thereby achieving Vito's unrealized dream for Michael? In other words, is 'Fredo' an insult because it exposes one's deeper insecurities and lays bare the unavoidable inequalities, which often inflict emotional damage, of the bourgeois family romance?

These kinds of dynamics lie behind the emotional turmoil portrayed in the HBO Max series *Succession* (2018-2023), which is patterned on *The Godfather* in its depiction of a successful entrepreneurial father with immigrant roots who has attained almost mythical status for his three sons and one daughter, all of whom fall short of the patriarch's expectations yet who ultimately remain firmly under his authoritarian grip. Updated to a contemporary context, one that is equally indebted to the biographies of Rupert Murdoch and Donald Trump families, the series retains the notion that masculine temperament and cunning are the foremost qualities that determine the rightful heir to a family-run enterprise (which, while more licit than that of the Corleone's, often reveals itself to be equally corrupt and distasteful). *Succession* appears to fulfil Coppola's appreciation of Puzo's novel *The Godfather* as "a story that was a metaphor for American capitalism in the tale of a great king with three sons" (Coppola 2016, 24).

The series begins with an introduction to a multinational media empire named Waystar RoyCo, which is the brainchild of its ruthless founder Logan Roy, a foulmouthed and unsentimental patriarch with little patience for his adult children. In the first episode it becomes evident that Roy's longstanding reign over his empire is at risk when he suffers a series of episodes that expose his diminishing physical and cognitive abilities. Against his will, even Roy recognizes that he must seek an eventual successor to his throne. Despite his lack of sentimentality, the principles of consolidation of wealth fuel his determination to have one of his own children take over the helm of the company, even though he is convinced that they are all preternaturally incapable of fulfilling the task.

While his temperament and demeanor are the antithesis of Vito Corleone, the character of Logan Roy is similarly vexed by the inability of his three sons to fulfil his ideals. Unlike the *Godfather*, *Succession* conjures Fredo not through one character alone but through an amalgamation of all the siblings who aspire to leadership and, perhaps more significantly, fatherly approval. The heir apparent is Kendall, who mirrors Fredo's lack of impulse control and inability to moderate his consumption of alcohol with his continuous struggles with drug addiction, his failed marriage, and his immoderate choices in business. Roy's eldest son Connor, a half-sibling of the other three siblings, is a slightly dimwitted millionaire who is engaged to a former call girl, and who is never once deferred to or allowed to participate in the family business as anything other than a shareholder. The youngest son

Roman, an insouciant upstart, is not seriously considered by his other siblings as a rival in the quest to take over as head of the family business. Although Roman proves himself to be cleverer than assumed, by the end of the series he appears to have inherited Fredo's emotional excesses when he creates a spectacle by hysterically weeping at his father's funeral, where he is so overcome by grief that he is unable to deliver the eulogy. Like Fredo, Roman is also associated with motherlove, reflected in his closer relationship with his somewhat distant mother as well as his inappropriate sexual obsession with Gerri, a maternal aunt-like figure. Roman is thus in a childlike, pre-Oedipal position, an element that is emphasized by the casting of the diminutive, baby-faced Kieran Culkin. When he is eventually passed over for the dynastic title, Roman responds not with anger but a paroxysm of emotion as he sobs, "Couldn't it have been me?" Yet his older brother Kendall too will ultimately be denied the seat of power, a birthright he desperately tries to invoke as he pleads in disbelief, "But I'm the eldest boy!," an echo of Fredo's admonition to Michael, "I'm your older brother, Mike, and I was stepped over!"

While *Succession*'s more overt borrowings from *The Godfather* trilogy are apparent, as is attested to by numerous critical reviews and commentaries on fan sites, it is more than just an homage to a great cinematic precedent. In its re-imagining of Fredo by means of distributing his foibles and disappointments amongst the offspring of an impressively powerful patriarch, the series is able to reflect on the insecurities that can characterize modern familial dynamics in the period of late capitalism. The show's depiction of fraternal competition, father-worship, and attention-seeking all take exaggerated forms that are to be derided, yet they may still be all-too familiar to viewers. Moreover, the emotional wounds that are exposed throughout the series demonstrate a warning that when family bonds are intertwined with corporate interests, the latter is poised to prevail.

CONCLUSION

The cases cited above are just a few prominent examples of the long reach that the Fredo archetype has on the popular conscious, and why more than half a century after John Cazale's remarkably nuanced interpretation of the character Fredo seems as relevant as ever. That Fredo is pathetic is indisputable; however, the multiple meanings of the term lend to divergent interpretations of his character. While the primary definition of pathetic, according to the OED, is something that arouses sadness, compassion, or sympathy, negative perceptions of Fredo favor the word's more colloquial interpretation, in which the pathetic is "[m]iserably inadequate; of such a low standard as to be ridiculous or contemptible."[4] Yet this disregards the Aristotelian conception of pathos within the drama, wherein the pathetic constitutes the highest elements of tragedy because it is that which appeals to the emotions. If pathos is intimately engaged with the feelings of the audience, therefore, all emotional content throughout the *Godfather* trilogy is inherently pathetic:

---

[4] https://www.oed.com/dictionary/pathetic_adj?tab=meaning_and_use #31758 389. Accessed September 28, 2023.

the senseless shooting through the heart of a lovelorn Mary Corleone; the image of the orphan child Vito Andolini singing to himself as he sits in confinement on Ellis Island; or indeed, the weeping of a devoted Fredo over the lifeless body of his father. Fredo's association with the emotional, therefore, it the key to reading the *Godfather* trilogy as a tension between pathos and the intellectual, rationale side that is associated with Michael and his criminal kingdom. By privileging Fredo in our readings we might find an even more searing indictment of the family under capitalism than originally thought.

BIBLIOGRAPHY

Coppola, Francis Ford. 2016. *The Godfather Notebook*. New York: Simon & Schuster.

Flynn, Meagan. 2019. "CNN's Chris Cuomo Threatened to Throw a Man Down Stairs for Calling Him 'Fredo,' Comparing it to the N-word." *Washington Post*, August 13. *Gale Academic OneFile* (accessed September 29, 2023).

The Godfather. 1972. Dir. Francis Ford Coppola. Paramount Pictures.

Kidwell, Roland E, Kimberley A. Eddleston, John James Cater III, and Franz W. Kellermanns. 2013. "How One Bad Family Member Can Undermine a Family Firm: Preventing the Fredo Effect." *Business Horizons* 56: 5-12.

Kidwell, Roland E, Franz W. Kellermanns, and Kimberley A. Eddleston. 2012. "Harmony, Justice, Confusion and Conflict in Family Firms: Implications for Ethical Climate and the 'Fredo Effect.'" *Journal of Business Ethics* 106:4: 503-517.

Puzo, Mario. 1969. *The Godfather*. New York: G. P. Putnam's Sons.

Tamburri, Anthony Julian. 2019. "Michael Corleone's Tie: Francis Ford Coppola's *The Godfather*." In *Mafia Movies: A Reader*, edited by Dana Renga, 70-75. Toronto: U Toronto P.

Fredo looks up at Micheal at their mother's funeral.

Festivals, Food, & Folklore
Foodways as a Politic of Representation
in *The Godfather*

RYAN CALABRETTA-SAJDER

Francis Ford Coppola's Godfather trilogy — *The God-father* (1972), *The Godfather Part II* (1974), and *The Godfather Part III* (1990) — has been and remains at the forefront of discussion amongst scholars and spectators alike since the original 1972 release.[1] Whether for its treatment of the mafia, its clever incorporation of Italian philosophical thought, or solely for Coppola's expert manipulation of the camera, the series has and will continue to capture the attention of viewers for its varied messaging and scaffolded interpretative nature. Scholars continue to discuss it as a capitalist manifesto on the American Dream myth or the story of a family. From a filmic perspective, *The Godfather* is truly a work of art, attested by the American Film Institute's ranking on the 100th greatest American films of all time, and will continue to capture the hearts of viewers for time to come.[2] Whether used in classroom or scholarly research, *The Godfather*

---

[1] It is also important to note that Francis Ford Coppola recently released *The Godfather, Coda: The Death of Michael Corleone* (2020), a new version of *The Godfather*, Part III (1990). Coppola changes the opening scene and closing scene, as well as some others. The reviews are mixed on the new version of the 1990 story.

[2] According to the American Film Institute, *The Godfather* is the second "Greatest American Film of All Time," next to *Citizen Kane* (1941). See, https://www.afi.com/afis-100-years-100-movies-10th-anniversary-edition/?gclid=Cj0KCQjwvLoBhCxARIsAHkOiu3OctOxMyaMNVid2Dq2vpIeSGtiEd6374-DyB9EBTvV9n8FB-nLowMaAiFeEALw_wcB.

series endures the test of time, offering both the informed and uninformed spectator of Italian American cinema newfound approaches of analysis.[3]

The Godfather series has received a plethora of scholarly attention over the years. Coppola and company have earned much deserved space within the field, from dedicated books and edited volumes to numerous book chapters and journal articles, crossing the gamut of academic fields. Yet, as much as there has been written on the topic, as this volume illustrates, there is still much left to consider. In this vein, I intend to explore the use of festivals, folklore, and foodways throughout *The Godfather* series. To be clear from the outset, when discussing "folklore," my intentions are to use folklore as a synonym for "tradition" and focus primarily on the traditional gender roles presented. Because this task is rather excessive for a shorter contribution, my goal is to share the outline of my approach, underscore some macrocosmic examples that can be seen throughout all three films, and finally explore my theoretical approach as seen in *The Godfather* through a handful of specific scenes to clearly illustrate my thesis.

Thus, I intend to explore the use of festivals, meals, and specific food items in the films through the narrative voice and the following motifs — narration, consolation, spectacle, collateral — arguing that foodways serves as a politic of representation. What do I mean when consider-

---

[3] For a thorough definition and the most salient example of Anthony Julian Tamburri's term the "informed spectator of Italian American cinema," see "What Does Scorsese Mean in *Mean Streets?*" in *Signing Italian/American Cinema: A More Focused Look* (2021). A clearer use of this concept will follow in this contribution.

ing the theory of foodways as a politic of representation? Foodways opens numerous discussions of violence either, or, precedes some type of mafia action, i.e., threat, revenge, murder. Therefore, foodways holds various roles within the film as it creates politics within the narrative, but often even outside of it. As Louise DeSalvo and Edvige Giunta have already demonstrated, foodways maintains a power dynamic, "Food, we had come to understand, played a particularly important part in defining modes of power within an Italian American domestic context" (1). Although DeSalvo and Giunta focus more on the point of view of female challenges, foodways claims authority overall.

As previously mentioned, scholars, critics, and spectators alike have argued the value and significance of the first film's release until the present.[4] Therefore, I am hardly the first scholar to note the significance of foodways in these films. In fact, at least eight critical articles have considered *The Godfather* series and foodways in some manner or in combination with other mafia or Italian American cinema. Some of the most recent pieces were published in 2021: "Cibo, dono, patria e famiglia: un approccio etno-antropologico a *The Godfather*" by Ermelinda Campani and "'Luca Brasi sleeps with the Fishes': The Gastromythology of *The Godfather* Trilogy" by Arup K. Chatterjee. Most scholars exploring food and *The Godfather* focus on gender and family,[5] the Italian-American

---

[4] Some include: Chris Messenger, George DeStefano, George S. Larke-Walsh, Peter Bondanella Nick Browne, and Jonathan J. Cavallero.
[5] I use the term "gender" in this phrase to reference traditional approaches to stereotyped gender roles within a family, i.e. the role of the female in the Italian American family.

myth, and/or capitalism.[6] One of the most interesting approaches, at least from a theoretical stance, is Chatterjee's piece, which examines the concept of *rasadhvani* in relationship to food in *The Godfather* series, underscoring its solely metaphoric nature, which in some ways returns to J. R. Keller's critical argument.

In fact, when exploring the concept of foodways within media studies, it is critical to remember what Keller reminds us:

> S/he has no access to the audience's palates, but can only invoke appetite and desire in a strictly visual and auditory medium, the most important ingredients in the gustatory experience — smell and taste — remaining inaccessible to the audience. Thus food can only even be a metaphor in film as it can never be consumed by the audience, save in visual or auditory sense. (3)

Keller's observation is formidable because it underscores the lack of power foodways has for the spectator. Film and media can only ever represent reality, so the metaphor

---

[6] See also Ira Torresi, 's "Identity in a Dish of Pasta: the Role of Food in the Filmic Representation of Italian-Americanness," Peter Naccarato's "There's a mobster in the kitchen: Cooking, eating, and complications of gender in *The Godfather* and *Goodfellas*," Steve Zimmerman's "Food in Films: A Star is Born," David Sutton and Peter Wogan's "The Gun, the Pen, and the Cannoli: Orality and Writing in *The Godfather, Part I*," Hafsa Rehman's "Female Identity in Gangster Movies: A Study of *The Godfather* Movie," Marlisa Santos's " ' Leave the Gun; Take the Cannoli': Food and Family in the Modern American Mafia Film," Martin Parker's "Eating with Mafia: Belonging and Violence," and Davide Girardelli's "Commodified Identities: The Myth of Italian Food in the United States."

and semiotic merit must suffice. However, I would argue that because of the lack of smell and taste for the spectator, the metaphorical significance in film assumes an even greater meaning as foodways communicates to us, particularly through the language of the camera. In fact, the use of the camera assumes a foundational role in interpreting the significance festivals, folklore, and foodways indeed maintain, thus underscoring its innate power and its politics of representation.

From a nurturing standpoint, the journalist Bunny Crumpacker reminds us that "Food is our first comfort, our first reward. Hunger is our first frustration" (3). In this manner, foodways plays a critical role in both the life cycle and the makeup of the family. As children, we have little control over feeding and thus must rely on family to feed us. Foodways can be seen as transactional as it builds upon relationships; even from the microcosmic, foodways asserts a power dynamic. Similarly, the sociologist Carole M. Counihan has argued that "eating gave the body not only pleasure but also consolation ... [Florentines] defined the body not as a product of personal moral concern but as a product of the family, given by nature through the family" (182). These concepts uphold a significant role in the use of foodways in *The Godfather* Trilogy. Foodways as consolation is, in fact, inherent in the Italian and Italian-American community and negotiates power and position, as DeSalvo and Giunta allude. As I will illustrate, food and wine brace the body emotionally to receive both positive and negative effects.

FOOD AS A NARRATIVE VOICE

From the narratological perspective, *The Godfather* Trilogy revolves around festivals. In fact, each film begins, and concludes, with a festival or special event. While the films work within a series, they maintain autonomy and present a circular nature, while simultaneously building a cyclical nature collectively. As *The Godfather* opens, the spectator is privy to Connie Corleone's wedding, and at the end, they experience Don Vito's funeral and, finally and most importantly, the Baptism of Connie's child. In *The Godfather Part II*, we witness the Corleone family move to Las Vegas and the Communion Party of his son, Anthony, in Lake Tahoe. Throughout the film, the spectator also witnesses the funeral of Vito Corleone's father, the San Rocco festival in Little Italy, and Vito Corleone's 50th birthday party through a flashback sequence. *The Godfather Part III* opens with Michael Corleone's induction into the Order of Saint Sebastian at St. Patrick's Old Cathedral. The final festival is Anthony's performance of *Cavalleria Rusticana* at the famous Teatro Massimo in Palermo, Sicily.

From a cyclical perspective, *The Godfather* presents Connie as a weak, docile wife and mother who only reacts to the males around her. In *The Godfather Part II*, we note a detached Connie who continues to react negatively to the situation she found herself in, "acting out," most notably sexually due to the murder of her husband. Yet, in *The Godfather Part III*, Connie evolves. Even though she maintains reactionary, she longs for power and joins the decision-making of the family business when Michael is unable.[7] She purposefully inserts herself into the politics of the business, and she, in fact, uses food to dominate. On the flip side, Anthony, Michael's son, preserves his innocence, first while witnessing his grandfather's death, then in the opening scene of *Part II* when we celebrate his communion in Lake Tahoe, and finally in *Part III* when he assumes a significant role within the opera world and denounces his study of law. Thus, these two characters demonstrate a gender role reversal, one of many examples in the series; considering Michael's past, we would expect Anthony to follow in his father's footsteps as he initially studies law and then abandons his study to pursue opera, as we learn in the beginning of *Part III*. Instead, Connie, and to a certain point Mary, assumes that role, which allows Anthony to pursue his passion for music and opera.

Festivals, thus, serve as a means of exploring growth, power, and political capital.[8] When considering Connie's wedding, various aspects come to light. It is important to return to the family photo. When Don Vito finally has a break and attempts to join the wedding feast, the family lines up for a group photo, and only then does he realize that Michael is missing. He refuses to document the moment without his youngest son, nicknamed by many the "war hero" due to his service in WWII. In fact, when Michael does indeed arrive, he is dressed in his military

---

[7] Connie's evolution is rather interesting and should be considered in a separate contribution. I do not think it is a clear black and white transformation, especially when considering *The Godfather Part II*.

[8] Although for a future paper, the entire St. Sebastian ceremony and award relates to Michael recycling money with the Vatican Bank.

uniform rather than a suit. Thus, Michael stands out from all the other men. First, all are wearing suits; secondly, most are wearing dark suits. Michael's army greens strike a stark contrast when he enters, even more so within the frame of the photo; Michael's "honest" presence seems like a forced afterthought. Yet, Michael's outfit is critical in understanding his importance within the family and, of course, his future. His character is supposed to represent the respectable lifestyle of honor, yet he fills the void left within his family and truly assumes his role as head of the family.[9] Michael's military outfit causes the spectator to connect differently; military dress is a reminder that he is "one of the good guys." To clarify the argument, he chooses to include Kay, probably the only non-Italian (besides the 'adopted' Tom Hagen) at the entire party. Remember, the political figures all sent their regrets. In this visual rendering, Michael sends a message to both the Corleones and us, the spectators. This sense of affect that his military attire produces continues our support for Michael, at least throughout the first film.

On the flip side, Michael's presence in the photo solidifies his future as Don; this is a visual foreshadowing of the narrative structure. While Michael denies his interest in assuming his father's business to Kay and repeats it twice, in the end, he justifies his father's business, arguing

---

[9] It is also important to remember that the military is Michael's first introduction to murder. Although laced in a positive sentiment, it is crucial to recall that Michael is first trained to be the protector of nation and then later morphs into the protection of family, and as such heritage. (Conversation with Anthony Julian Tamburri and Abel Fenwick at the IASA Conference, Oct. 26-29, 2023, at the University of Arkansas, Fayetteville).

that the mafia world is equally bad, or better, than the political one.[10] In his brief monologue lecturing Kay, he justifies intent with a straight face, convinced of what he says. Although outside the purview of foodways, Michael's early presentation highlights his "otherness" and embodies Don Vito's desire for him to rise above organized crime, preferring his son to write and administer the law rather than break it.

When exploring the festivals as a narrative device, we learn early in *The Godfather* that there is a line of people waiting to meet Don Vito Corleone to ask for a favor. If the spectator is unaware of that tradition, it is repeated three times. First and foremost, Don Vito reminds Bonasera that he will grant him his request, even if with hesitation, as part of the tradition on his daughter's wedding day. We also hear a similar tale when Tom Hagen kisses his wife and returns inside to assist Don Vito with his visitors. Before leaving, he whispers into his wife's ear, explaining that the Don cannot deny any request on his daughter's wedding day, hence why he, as *consigliere,* is so busy. Finally, the promised tradition is alluded to when Luca Brasi is practicing his speech alone at a table, waiting his turn to meet Don Vito. Michael and Kay are sitting together chatting, and Kay inquiries about the odd man speaking to himself; Michael reveals the story

---

[10] Visually, this moment is noteworthy as the spectator can connect Michael's dress to that of the "modern" mobster. Although he never assumes the fashion sense of his father, Michael transforms from being one with the U.S. government to one with the Mafia. For further discussions on this topic, see Anthony Julian Tamburri's chapter in this volume.

of Johnny Fontane. These three moments justify the communal nature of an Italian wedding. Ironically, Luca is not in line to make a request. Rather, he only wants to thank Don Vito for the invitation to his daughter's wedding; he was surprised to be invited. This act stands out, demonstrating to both the Don and the spectator Luca's loyalty to the family. It is of little surprise, then, when Luca is asked to falsely infiltrate Sollozzo's clan.

Additionally, the concept of foodways and festivals serves as a means of chronological narratology. In theory, Connie's wedding is a celebration of love and family; Connie and Carlo immediately begin a new life together. Carlo longs to enter the family business. In fact, Tom Hagen assumes that Don Vito would like to assign him an important role. Rather, he suggests a much less important one, in which Carlo never understands the intricacies of the family business. As we know, Connie becomes pregnant quickly after marriage and then prepares to Baptize her child. After the burial of Don Vito, Michael assumes complete control of the family reins and then can act as he chooses.

Michael purposefully and cleverly manipulates the most critical of all Catholic celebrations, the Baptism, to illustrate his own dominance over both family and the mafia world of NYC. As he both verbally and visually confirms his allegiance to God through the sacred Trinity, the spectator witnesses the assassination of the heads of all five New York families in a series of cuts, from Michael responding "I do" within the church to the slaughter of a family boss. Through an amazing manipulation of the camera, many murders are seen through the point of view of the assassin, highlighting the murderous aspect but also sharing the point of view with the spectator, which also includes us in the action. The best and most intense is the assassination of Moe Greene, discussed later. Another compelling example is the murder of the mob boss in bed. Both scenes share a point of view shot placing us in the "monster's" seat. The other murders, instead, are diverse. One assumes a shot-reverse-shot in the revolving door, which also proves interesting. In the revolving door scene, the spectator experiences more emotion, as we see both expressions of murderer and murdered. This type of shot not only creates tension for the spectator, but also, this medium shot underscores the powerful and powerless. Thus, the individual murder scenes in and of themselves are marvelously shot, as most bring to the forefront a shot-reverse-shot stylistic movement, again underscoring the power of Michael on his clan.

Although not laced in foodways per se, Coppola uses the concept of festival to create a narrative voice. Michael's crew is not injured at all, and the ambushes illustrate his clever nature over his opponents. Visually, the camera reveals the hierarchical structure of *la cosa nostra* as Michael remains "innocent" in the church, participating in the most important of all Catholic ceremonies, Baptism, where the child is claimed innocent and able to begin life free from sin. Michael also renews his own vows, as is typical with all present at a Baptism, yet, simultaneously plays "god" with others' lives, underscoring a newfound comfort in his overt role, as well as his covert one. Michael's control over his crew is marvelous as each capo assassinates a family head.

Moreover, one of the most obvious interpretations of this festival scene is that Michael plays god. First, he murders all the heads of the five families, regaining the control that his father previously maintained. Secondly, he asserts his power over his family, assuming the spiritual role of Godfather to Connie's firstborn. Lastly, he manipulates Connie directly and moves to murder her husband. In this regard, we note that festivals function to narrate and create spectacle; each assignation in this scene is spectacular — one more so than the next. One clear example is the assassination of Moe Greene. Moe did not want to "see" nor accept the power of the Corleone family, as he was already in dialogue with Barzini, so his sight was taken from him before he was killed.

FOOD AS A CONSOLING AFFECT

As Carole Counihan has noticed in her research with foodways and Italians, foodways functions on the level of consolation. There are numerous moments throughout *The Godfather* in which food assumes a ritual of consolation. We see this concept very early on, which can be easily overlooked as the scene generally holds much more weight within the film. Bonasera attempts to justify to Don Vito why he chose to trust the police rather than the mafia for justice. Don Vito retorts quickly, "I can't remember the last time you invited me to your house for a cup of coffee," underscoring the fact that Bonasera has never invited the Don over to his house, not even for a coffee, even though his wife is godmother to Bonasera's child. Although a simple example shared in passing, Don Vito illustrates how food assists in consolation and relationship building. Don Vito questions Bonasera's intentions, as well as his loyalty because even though they are "family," at least through the church, Bonasera attempts to be the integrated US migrant, afraid to owe the godfather favors or be involved with illegal activity. Yet in the end, Bonasera returns to the godfather and his politics, desperate, during the wedding feast, evidencing my argument on two levels: food as collateral and food as consolation.

A similar moment occurs when Sonny is killed at the toll booth. Don Vito is still recovering at home, and Tom must break the news of his son's death. The Don knows something is wrong because he confronts Tom about the weeping of his wife. Before breaking the bad news, however, Don Vito requests Tom to pour him a drink to prepare him for the coming news. Tom serves his Don a drink and then shares the sad news. Before drinking, the Don acknowledges the need to have a drink to calm his nerves and prepare himself for the negative announcement; therefore, his drink attempts to console him. We can interpret the significance of wine in a few ways. On the surface, Don Vito prepares himself for bad news by drinking a glass of wine to calm his nervous, sensing the gravitas of the situation to come. Yet in Egypt and the ancient Mediterranean, wine accompanied the burial of the body as it created a sense of community and a connection to society. It was buried to escort the body in its journey in the afterlife.[11] Although Sonny is not buried with wine, there is a

---

[11] For a more robust history of wine, see "The symbolism of wine in history." https://www.lev2050.com/en/the-symbolism-of-wine-in-history/.

short of toast to a better afterlife within this and the next scene. Wine also symbolizes transformation — in this scene, we observe a variety of transformations: Sonny passes away, the Don becomes emotional, and eventually Michael returns to supervise the family business.[12] Finally, within the Christian tradition, wine reminds us of sacrifice; Catholics believe that the wine during the Mass goes through transubstantiation and becomes the Blood of Christ. Through this tradition, then, wine is sacrificial as it awakens in us the religious connotations of sacrifice. Sonny is sacrificed, which in theory allows Michael to return and seize the family power.

In the final scenes of *The Godfather,* Michael begins to settle all scores within the family, first with Tessio, who tries to get out of it, and later with Carlo. Michael enters a very dark house where Carlo is dialing a number on the telephone. When Michael enters, Carlo hangs up. Michael confronts Carlo about scheming with Barzini's clan and Carlo begs for his life (not forgiveness!). Michael requests that Carlo admit what he did, yet he never does. Michael insists that Carlo drink to settle his nerves. Michael tells Carlo that he won't make Connie a widow and will send him to Vegas, persisting in discovering who approached Carlo for this deal. Once Michael hears it was Barzini, he takes the glass of wine out of Carlo's hands and sends him on his way. Michael uses wine to both console and convince. Through comforting Carlo a bit, Michael achieves his goal — Carlo admits, albeit indirectly,

---

[12] See, "Wine Symbolism & Meaning (Friendship & Gluttony) https://symbolismandmetaphor.com/wine-symbolism-meaning/.

being a traitor, and Michael confirms his suspicion. Captured in a two shot, aimed at creating some sort of trust between Michael and Carlo, some spectators may believe at first that Carlo is indeed safe. But as the next scene demonstrates, Carlo is not free.

One of the most compelling examples of food as consolation comes towards the end of the film, outside the Don's garden, which is in full bloom. The moment, underscored with the abundant garden, denotes the final transfer of power from Don Vito to what then becomes Don Michael.[13] While outside chatting, the Don shares his last bit of wisdom with Michael before the Don's death regarding Barzini and a meeting. He later apologizes to Michael for overthinking the current situation, stating, "I spent my life trying not to be careless. Women and children can be careless, but not men." Before this moment, he talks about wine, "I like to drink more than I used to. Anyway, I'm drinking more." Don Vito shares how he envisioned a diverse trajectory for Michael and concluded, "Don't forget, whoever organizes the meeting is the traitor." Until his dying day, Don Vito aims to protect his family and train Michael to properly assume the reins.

Once again, we observe how the Don, dressed in brown clothing, opens up to Michael personally and professionally while consuming a glass of wine. It is probably one of the most personal moments the Don shares with any other character within the film. In this dialogue, he also tries to comfort Michael, as this will become one of his first major decisions as don.

---

[13] See, Devin Mainville. "A Great Display of Florals in *The Godfather*."

Foodways also supplements and maintains the Italian-American cultural myth in many ways. Although others have written about it, it is important to underscore a few examples. Returning to the opening scene, the grandiose nature of the wedding is one simple example. Additionally, there is a moment when Clemenza dances and calls for Paulie to give him some wine. Paulie obeys, returns, and hands Clemenza a jug of red wine, from which he drinks directly. Clemenza thus embodies the Italian-American myth of being obese, gross, and overeating. In the scene, he is sweating, dancing, eating, and drinking; he presents all the negative aspects of the gluttonous Italian-American man. Still within the opening wedding scene, Paulie is seen with a bunch of Italian submarine sandwiches, listing the lunch meats off in Italiese, adding to the gluttonous Italian-American stereotype.

FOOD AS SPECTACLE

Additionally, I argue that food serves as a spectacle. As a whole, foodways in and of itself entices the spectator. Two particular scenes come to mind. First, Connie's wedding serves as a spectacle. At the wedding feast, we have various situations unfolding. We first experienced Bonasera and the intimate requests of Don Vito's guests. Then, we are serenaded by Johnny Fontane and later by Mama Corleone and another guest, singing "Luna Mezzo Mare" on a stage in front of the entire wedding.[14]

Moreover, while the party is happening within the compound, another party is occurring outside the family's

---

[14] The lyrics and connotations present in the song have sexual undertones and deserve to be analyzed in relation to this scene.

walled and gated entrance. Right outside the property, we see a group of FBI officers with cameras snapping photos of all the license plates of the mobsters. Sonny, hot-headed as usual, confronts the FBI, grabs the camera, throws it to the ground, destroys the evidence, and throws some cash at them to cover the cost of the damage. Here, both festival and food come together to draw the attention of the FBI. This scene establishes how the feast creates both internal and external affect. This event brings a large community of the underworld from outside the family into the same space and place, enticing law enforcement to "attend" and poke around to gather intel. From inside the family, the Corleone men react diversely to food and the party.

Although seen in passing, Enzo the baker's creation assumes center stage for 30 seconds. While asking the godfather for his favor, he shares with grand excitement the beautiful cake he prepared for Connie's wedding. The cake is processed into the party, almost like a statue of a saint in a religious procession and demonstrates the baker's loyalty to his don. The grandness and height of the cake, at least four tiers high, maybe five, provides a phallic presentation to the guests, illustrating its ancient Greek and Roman roots: "As part of the nuptials, the groom broke bread over the bride's head. This was to symbolize her submission, the end of her purity, and to represent good luck and fertility" (MobileAssociate). At first, Connie does in fact become submissive, cooking and cleaning for Carlo while he entertains diverse mistresses, yet eventually in *Part II* and *Part III*, Connie comes into her own.

The wedding feast also encourages actions within the sexual realm. Sonny's wife catches him cruising one of the women in Connie's wedding party early on. Sonny tells her to watch the kids, and she quickly retorts, "watch yourself." Later, Sonny changes seats to move closer to this woman and continues to flirt. The camera cuts to frame Sonny's wife chatting with a group of girlfriends demonstrating how large Sonny's penis is. No sooner does Sonny's wife look over her shoulder to check on him than he's gone with the bridesmaid to have sex. Thus, food serves as an aphrodisiac, especially for Sonny, as we see him overtly pursuing the bridesmaid even when his father requests his presence. Moreover, his family, in particular his father and Tom Hagen, allow him to continue his extramarital affairs. Full of pride, Sonny doesn't even care about the possibility of being caught or disrespecting his wife. Rather, he openly acts. His wife, on the other hand, brags about his masculinity as she visually demonstrates the length of Sonny's penis. The visual image connects Italian imagery, although never verbally communicated. As Sonny's wife brags about her husband's member, one may easily think of an Italian sausage. Moreover, her visual representation of Sonny's penis causes a spectacle — she is framed in a medium shot with her girlfriends surrounding her — framed with a pitcher of wine and an orange directly in front of her. She takes her hands and starts shorter and continually increases the length until she concludes. Then she looks around at her girlfriends and they all laugh in unison, highlighting how Sonny's penis becomes a wedding spectacle for them to enjoy, while in reality the only woman truly enjoying it is the bridesmaid. Here food serves in two ways, maybe — in vino veritas for Sonny's penis and the orange reminds us of his virility as he literally exits the scene to engage in sexual activity.

FOOD AS COLLATERAL, MAFIA STYLE?

Once again, we turn to our friend Bonasera, who desperately attempts to become American. In fact, it is one of the first words he says in his speech to Don Vito. While we do not need to spend much more time analyzing the character of Bonasera, again, we see Bonasera's relationship with Don Vito as completely transactional. Even though Bonasera finally calls Don Vito by his title and agrees to conduct a favor if called upon, we understand that Bonasera is uncomfortable and not "willingly" accepting. Instead, he is desperate and wants "justice" for his daughter. Not inviting Don Vito over postponed any type of collateral that may have existed; through this relationship, we note the struggle between the Old World and the New World mentality. Bonasera longs to integrate into American society, leaving behind traditional Italian society, yet he is forced to return to Old World norms, i.e., returning to the godfather's table and requesting a favor. As such, Don Vito was disrespected and hesitant to assist when Bonasera truly needed it. Thanks to the tradition of not denying any request on his daughter's wedding day, Bonasera's wish did come true, demonstrating how the Old World still dominates in the New World.[15] Although not the primary focus of this contribution, *The Godfather* represents the migrant

---

15 For a semiotic understanding of the conceptualization of Old World vs. New World, see, Tamburri (2011).

struggle from the Old World to the New World, which is one reason scholars flock to exploring the Marxist/capitalist discourse present within the narrative.

THE (IN)FAMOUS ORANGE

A second moment in which food plays a collateral role is when Tom goes to visit Jack Woltz from the production studio. Tom is invited to the house, where they drink and see the grounds, including meeting Tartum, Woltz's prized horse. After touring the grounds, Tom and Woltz dine together. Initially fine, Woltz gets upset and eventually throws Tom out. Before that moment, we observe a bowl of oranges in the center of the table, a fruit that maintains significant symbolism throughout the film. In fact, this is not the first time we see an orange within the film narrative. Very slyly, as the camera pans during Connie's wedding, Tessio is captured with an orange. As numerous film scholars, journalists, and others have noted, the orange foreshadows death or tragedy.[16] Although Coppola and team claim the oranges were added for color, one can read the metaphoric meaning on diverse levels. As Chiara Mazzucchelli argued at the conference which produced this volume, the oranges remind us of Sicily and the Corleones' Sicilian roots.[17] Moreover, due to its shape and color, the orange reminds us of the sun. While some film scholars have accepted Dean Tavoularis's statement, "oranges were simply another carefully chosen compliment to otherwise somberly dressed set. 'We knew this

---

[16] See, Ben Sherlock, *"The Godfather*: Why the Oranges Are So Important."
[17] See, Chiara Mazzucchelli's chapter in this volume.

film wasn't going to be about bright colors, and oranges make a nice contrast.'" (Tavoularis in Harlen Lebo), many have not. When exploring the significance of oranges historically and through the cultural lens of the Mediterranean, we are reminded that they represent fertility and change.[18]

It is hard to deny a connection between the orange and death. As previously mentioned, the abundant bowl of oranges graces Woltz's table as they dine. The allusion is clearly in front of Woltz before he becomes upset and confronts Tom directly. If what Chiara Mazzucchelli suggests is true, the orange brings us back to *Sicilianità;* then, unfortunately, we also align Sicily with the Mafia, which is a subtheme of the film, one of which Woltz is aware of as he claims not to be threatened by the Don, knowing Johnny Fontane's story. We recall that each episode in the series has a strong and direct relationship with the *madre terra.* We also understand that the Corleone men cannot survive in their native Sicily; they are never safe. Thus, the beauty of the citrus simultaneously reminds the spectator of one's own mortality. Although not analyzed here, one of the final images within the entire series is Michael keeling over in a chair outside his villa in Sicily, dead, having just dropped an orange. The orange sits at the dead man's feet, still moving, slightly rolling, while Michael finally meets his maker.

To return for a minute to Connie's wedding, Tessio is the first to be seen with an orange, and as the film progresses, we learn that he is the final traitor collaborating with Barzini. Moreover, unlike the various mafiosi through-

---

[18] See, Jesse Brauner. "What's the Meaning of Orange 'Fruit'."

out the series who take their punishment appropriately, Tessio tries to negotiate with Tom when he fears for his life. Thus, the informed Italian-American reader would immediately be aware of the foreshadowing of the orange, and by Tessio's death, even the attuned spectator would be.[19] In the film narrative, the orange warns us about Woltz's and Tessio's future.

But does the orange function in the same manner for Don Vito? The first direct encounter with the orange for our Don is when Sollozzo and company try to assassinate him. The Don purchases some oranges at a street market, and when he realizes a group of men are coming to kill him, he runs, knocking oranges over into the street as well as losing the grip on his own bag of oranges and having them spill into the street. As we know, Don Vito survives this attempt on his life. At this point in the film, however, one cannot argue that oranges necessarily equate to death unless we explore the film from a more metaphorical perspective.

In the penultimate scene of Vito's life, Vito has a heart-to-heart discussion with Michael, pouring his emotions and desired goals for his future. Vito wanted Michael to be the change in the legal world, not the underworld, underscored by his pride in Michael's service to his country. From the moment of the attack on Don Vito's

---

[19] See Anthony Julian Tamburri's "Visuality and Its [Dis]Contents: Looking Backward in Order to Move Forward" and "Signing Italian/American Cinema, Code-switching in the City: What Does Scorsese Mean in *Mean Streets?*" in *Signing Italian/American Cinema: A More Focused Look* to more fully understand his argument on the theoretical construction of the "informed" Italian American reader.

life, Michael is "forced" into the mafioso world of his father. In fact, one can analyze the slow evolution of Michael's entry into it through space, place, and light. If the orange, then, must represent death, it is Michael's death that it warrants. The reference is not physical, but it is all-encompassing, as from this moment forward, Michael only makes decisions based on the "Family" with a capital "F." Michael's deep love and respect for his father brings him full circle into the Family without hesitation. Only later, once he loses his true love, Apollonia, and returns to the US post-Sollozzo, does Michael truly grasp the underpinnings of the Family. In this reading of the film, then, the orange serves as a double-edged sword in the early part of *The Godfather*: while the orange may signify death, it represents Michael's future in the "honest" world; the orange is additionally a symbol of fertility and will in the end outlive Michael.

The orange, however, continues to have meaning for Don Vito. In his last scene, he is playing with an orange. He peels it, puts it in his mouth, and scares little Anthony, his grandson. As he chases Anthony with the orange in his mouth, it seems he becomes winded, but the Don has a heart attack in front of Anthony. Anthony, innocent and not understanding the situation, takes the pesticide gun his grandfather was playing with and uses it on Don Vito while he is dying on the ground. The image of the pesticide gun is powerful — Anthony kills the weeds surrounding his grandfather. As we see Anthony mature, he is always leery of the mafia and the issues the mafia brings to the table. We remember the shooting of the Lake Tahoe residence in *Part II* and his official break from the Family/family business in *Part III*.

Luca Brasi is chosen to entice the Tattaglia family acting as a traitor. When he arrives at the bar, which is almost completely dark and recalls a "man cave," as Donna Chirico describes, Sollozzo randomly appears to negotiate terms of changing teams.[20] The first thing asked is if Luca would like a scotch, to which he quickly refuses. Sollozzo and Brasi speak completely in Italian during their negotiations, and as soon as Luca agrees to join Sollozzo and Tattaglia, they treat him like an animal and assassinate him — they jam a knife through his hand, keeping him attached to the bar where he refused service and then someone pops out from behind and strangles him with a wire until his eyes practically pop out from their sockets. This method of murder is extremely animalistic as he is, to a certain extent, spit roasted as he is unable to move. Moreover, from a Lacanian lens, Luca is completely demasculinized as someone comes from behind and strangles him; Luca is placed in the passive position while his murderer is active, and his murderer does not just strangle Luca but wraps a wire completely around his throat, practically tying him up. Lastly, the spectator is forced to assume the point of view of the barkeeper, observing this entire process and unable to react or help. We are almost forced to side with team Sollozzo and Tattaglia at this moment. Although we know that Luca is not a traitor, his murder does remind us of the historical types of death provided to traitors within *La cosa nostra*, rendered with the

---

[20] See, Donna Chirico's chapter in this collection.

use of the wire and being "tied" up, first to the bar and later around his throat.

If his death is not enough to disturb both the spectator and the Corleone family, we learn that he has been disposed of in the sea, following a Sicilian tradition in which the older gentlemen, Clemenza and Tessio, need to explain to the new generation — Luca Brasi sleeps with the fishes.[21] While the message seems clear, what exactly does it mean? First, it is used as a threat to the Corleone family, demonstrating not only the power but also the cleverness — Sollozzo and Tattaglia immediately call bullshit on Brasi's fake traitorship, sending the message that they are one step ahead. Second, sleeping with the fishes signifies that Luca's death will always remain hidden since there will never be a body, which, from an ethical situation, is miserable. Lastly, however, Luca practically becomes fish food. The creatures of the sea will consume his body. Here, there is a flip of my critical use of food. Instead of food being collateral for Luca, Luca's life and body become the food and serve as collateral damage for a botched idea. Luca becomes a sacrificial lamb for the Corleones — although loyal to a fault, he becomes consumed and forgotten.

---

[21] The origin of this phrase is arguable. The idea is clearly present in Book 21 of Homer's *The Iliad*; however, this was not translated into English probably until the Thomas Hobbes translation of 1676. A similar expression exists in Richard Cumberland's *The Observer — Being a Collection of Moral, Literary, and Familiar Essays* (1785). Finally, we note it in Edmund Spencer's *Travels in Circassia, Krim-tartary, &c Including a Steam Voyage Down the Danube, from Vienna to Constantinople, and Round the Black Sea, in 1836. II. Volume 1.* See Liam Porter, "What Does 'Sleeping with the Fishes' Mean?"

One of the most cited scenes in *The Godfather* is when revenge is taken out on Paulie, who is responsible for the attack on Don Vito. Immediately following Luca's death, Clemenza is tasked with Paulie's vengeful murder. Clemenza, another colleague, and Paulie run errands all day, and eventually, Clemenza asks Paulie to pull over to urinate in the middle of nowhere. While Clemenza pees, his colleague shoots Paulie in the back of the head three times. It seems important to remind the viewer of the religious significance of three — the Trinity — as one bullet to the back of the head would have sufficed Paulie's death. Moreover, the death occurs in the middle of the countryside, but again, not necessarily in a random spot, as Paulie dies in the middle of a wheat field. While one meaning of wheat is that of mystery, which, to a certain level, functions even here since Paulie's death becomes mysterious and his motive for turning on Don Vito is never truly brought to life, wheat, like the oranges, serves as a symbol of fertility.[22] Additionally, it reminds us of resurrection and rebirth. With Paulie's death, the Corleone family has a rebirth of sorts, leading to a change in Family leadership. As Paulie's goal was to participate, even indirectly, in the assassination of Don Vito, in the film's narrative, the opposite occurs; Don Vito gets better and eventually resumes control of the Family. Yet, this action activates another momentum — the upward movement of what slowly becomes Michael's path to power, which I argue is a true rebirth of the Family. Thus, the

---

[22] The Editors of Give Me History. "The Symbolism of Wheat (Top 14 Meanings)."

location where Paulie is killed is critical for the food as collateral and narrative readings.

Yet, we can't forget the cannoli, as Clemenza's wife reminds us when he leaves for his busy day. The cannoli has numerous meanings. On the most basic level, the cannoli is a family treat. Clemenza follows his wife's orders and brings them home to appease her. The cannoli, which has roots in Sicily, reunites us with an earlier argument about the *Sicilianità* in *The Godfather*. Through foodways, these references unite the migrant/diasporic experience. Whether in Italy or the US, one would never grab a cannolo from a random bakery or restaurant; rather, one would always frequent a Sicilian one. Thus, cannoli bridge the Old World versus New World discourse, demonstrating a relationship that the migrant can never truly escape. Today these bakeries still attract Italians from the neighborhood and remain popular socio-political centers where everyone speaks in their dialect, the line accumulates at the door, and cash is the only form of payment. These bakeries are frequented weekly by many and become especially central to parties like weddings and similar events. Thus, even today, they maintain political power in the community.

When considering cannoli on a sexual level, they represent the phallus, which Clemenza metaphorically maintains. Clemenza is the brawn of the Family. While he does not kill Paulie directly, Paulie falls under his responsibility. The spectator observes Clemenza's hands physically clean of the murder, but he organizes the spectacle and observes it happening, even if we never share his point of view. Again, the manner in which Paulie is assassinated demonstrates the virility our symbolic cannoli maintain. Don't forget, it is the murderer who grabs the cannoli from the car after killing Paulie.

One of *The Godfather*'s most noted food scenes is the first of two bonding scenes between Michael and Clemenza. Clemenza consciously builds a relationship with Michael in these two scenes, one dealing with food, the second with weaponry. In the first scene, Michael is called inside to respond to Kay's phone call. Surrounded by men in what seems to be a "man cave," Michael listens to Kay say she loves him, waiting for a similar response. Embarrassed due to his environment, he evades defining his love while Clemenza pokes fun at him. Immediately after, Clemenza states:

> Come over here kid. Learn somethin'. You never know, you might have to cook for twenty guys someday. You see, you start up with a little water, then you fry some garlic. Then you throw in some tomatoes, tomato paste. You fry it. You make sure it doesn't stick. You get it to a boil. You shove in all your sausage and your meatballs. Add a little bit wine, and, a little bit of sugar. And that's my trick.

Michael follows Clemenza's instructions in this dark man cave but only watches; he does not take part. Sonny enters and says to both Michael and Clemenza that he has more important things for them to do, suggesting that cooking isn't a role for men, as their responsibilities remain elsewhere. Clemenza does not respond, continuing to make his sauce, demonstrating his comfort in assuming a diverse gender role from what may be expected of a typical capo. For Clemenza, the concept of family and togetherness counts, as he takes pride in cooking for his colleagues, as his sing-song tone of voice illustrates, paired with his excitement to teach a skill to Michael. Michael, in return, respects Clemenza, as the camera captures both of them, side by side, in a two shot. Coppola's use of the two shots illustrates the father-son-like bonding occurring between the two. Michael is fixed on the sauce and provides Clemenza the respect requested. This interior space is male-dominated, and the blinds are shut so their privacy is maintained. Even more, the light is particular — yellow hue rather than white — underscoring an atmosphere of ambiguity and mystery. It's a space for male bonding. Thus, on the one hand, it is odd that Clemenza assumes tasks traditionally confined to the female role, yet on the other hand, it makes complete sense as we do not see women allowed.

The other scene in which Clemenza and Michael bond concerns the gun. While not in the kitchen, they meet in another "man cave" where there are pin-ups of women and saints, tools, and other man-cave realia. Clemenza is prepping the gun for Michael, and he wants Michael to test it out. In this scene, we learn how proud Vito was of his service and how the entire Family supported him. The two men also tease each other over the gun, the symbol of both power and virility.

Although not directly related to foodways, Enzo the baker, who we meet at Connie's wedding, is the only non-family member to attempt to visit the Don in the hospital. Enzo, loyal to his Don, wants to pay his respects to the

Don and brings him flowers, yet Michael must create a new plan as he realizes Sollozzo's men are coming back to kill Don Vito. Michael sends Enzo outside to act as one of Don Vito's men and scare the other clan from attempting any wrongdoing. While the introduction to Enzo the baker serves as a request, and then the baking and presentation of a spectacular cake, in return, Enzo helps save Vito's life. Ironically, the baker does more than provide nourishment and delight. He also can pretend to be someone he isn't and protect the man who saved his daughter's relationship.

Even before Michael's entry on the mafioso stage, the Corleone men, along with the capos are dining at the Corleone home. The scene, presenting only men who are not sitting around a dining room table, as in other scenes; rather once again, they are in a sort of den, representative again of a "man cave" dark, with little light, setting the stage for Old World politics. Sharing a meal amongst only men underscores their work environment. They are not eating a traditional Mama Corleone meal, but Chinese take-out and beer. Half the men are jacket-less, except for Michael, Clemenza, and one other colleague. Sonny is shirtless, wearing only his undershirt and suspenders. All are waiting to hear from their secret informant about where the Sollozzo-McCluskey-Michael meeting will occur.

While we are not at all surprised that the men have returned to one of the many "man caves," at the Corleone residence, the choice of Chinese food is noteworthy as it stands out in the scene as untraditional. We are far from Clemenza teaching Michael the value of caring for the men through food. Here we notice a group of anxious men, worried about the future of the Family. Eventually, Sonny receives the call stating where the meet-up will happen. The camera captures Sonny in a full, then medium shot, as he walks towards the camera and resumes his position next to Michael, who again is dressed in a suit and ready to murder Sollozzo and McCluskey. In this medium shot with both brothers, accentuated with the Chinese food surrounding them, we sense not only the passing of power from Sonny to Michael (as Michael avenges his father) but also a step towards the New World, which in theory Michael represents, from the Old one.

When Michael begins his entrance into the family, he is tasked with killing both Sollozzo and McCluskey as his "initiation." They end up at an Italian restaurant in the Bronx and the first question McCluskey asks is, "How's the Italian food in this restaurant?" Sollozzo quickly responds, "Try the veal. It's the best in the city.", to which the officer responds, "I'll have it." The irony of McCluskey's question demonstrates his complete ignorance of the world he is trying to enter. An Italian would never bring another to a "bad" Italian restaurant. The waiter opens the bottle of wine and pours it. Sollozzo passes the first glass to Michael, almost as a peace offering. In theory, the wine should make everyone at the time calmer. The wine foreshadows the blood of Sollozzo and McCluskey, which will soon be spilled. The loud sound made from the popping of the cork conditions the viewer for the gunshots to come. The wine then becomes a spectacle as it produces a sense of sound and conditions the evening's dinner.

Moreover, after this question, Sollozzo begins to speak again, illustrating his "otherness" from the group. Lastly,

Sollozzo and Michael sit beside each other as Sollozzo again tries to create a bond with Michael. These actions create the affect that Sollozzo is attempting to win Michael over. In fact, when speaking in Italian/Sicilian, Michael becomes so overwhelmed and angry that he resorts to English. This code-switching by Michael is not a lack of knowledge; we know this because, in the next scene, Michael is sent to Sicily and can speak on a communicative level. Rather, Michael ends up in defense mode to protect his father and switches to English. This code-switching can be interpreted as Michael representing the New World, one moving away from Italian/Sicilian and moving into English in the US.

When Michael returns from the bathroom, Sollozzo continues to preach to him about what his father must do. At a certain point, when there is a lot of added noise from the subway, Michael stands up, looks Sollozzo directly in the eyes, and shoots him once square in the head. Then he pivots and does the same to McCluskey, first shooting him in the throat and then in the head.

The placement of the shots is meaningful. Sollozzo, who is the brains of the operation, is shot first, once through the head, demonstrating the importance of taking him out immediately. Moreover, it was Sollozzo who planned all the attacks as well as continually bothered Michael during the entire meal. Next, Michael takes his revenge on McCluskey, who more than deserves it. He is the only one eating at the table. As he piles his veal in his mouth, Michael first attacks his throat, then his head. From a semiotic interpretation, therefore, one can read McCluskey's death as gluttonous as he throws his hands around his throat and chokes to death on his veal. An Irish cop, McCluskey happily skimmed from the mafia to help protect them. By taking advantage of the Italian and Italian American community, McCluskey "lined his pockets" with the Italian dirty money. Ironically or not, McCluskey ends up in an Italian-American restaurant where he thinks his future will be sealed — a more lucrative relationship with Sollozzo, Tattaglia, and the Corleones. Instead, our war hero goes rogue, defending his father and his family's future. In this vein, we see that food inspires Michael to act, simultaneously destroying both Sollozzo and McCluskey.

Later in the film when Vito returns home from the hospital, Mama Corleone is cooking for the entire family. Although only mentioned in a whisper among others speaking, she says she is making chicken cacciatore. Historically, from the 14th to 16th centuries, "cacciatore" was a meal, often a stew, aimed to fill the stomachs of men on the hunt for large animals that would last their families awhile.[23] The idea was to nourish the hunters to find bigger and better game. This meal proves pertinent to the table talk at hand. First, Sonny, our acting Don, just finished an argument with Tom about taking out Tattaglia, to which Tom is completely contrary. Yet, Sonny longs for more power, authority, respect from the others, but in fact Tom knows that Sonny is a loose cannon and not grounded like his father. So, this meal fuels Sonny for more battles to come when he leaves abruptly to protect his sister and is eventually gunned down at the toll booth.

---

[23] Linda Lum, "The History of Chicken Cacciatore (and Five Recipes)."

At this cacciatore dinner, Sonny begins talking business at the table. Connie quickly scolds him, sharing that
Don Vito never did such a thing; he never mixed business
and pleasure. When Carlo degrades her for her comment,
Sonny protects her. Carlo then offers opinions on the Family business, and Sonny shuts him down, citing Connie.
Thus, we observe Carlo trying to get his own "hunt," which
would give him more family power. Yet Sonny quickly fore-
sees Carlo's ambition and squashes it. Although Sonny can
"eat" the little guy, Sonny will soon be eaten by a larger
hunter. Sonny does not create any capital or collateral and
remains blocked due to his ignorance and temper.

When we finally see Michael after the murders, he
appears literally walking through the Sicilian countryside amongst the olive trees. Michael walks aimlessly
through the countryside in a series of various shots: pan-
oramas, traveling, etc. First, we see him wandering, and
Don Tommasino approaches him in his car, informing
him to be careful because his enemies may know where
he is hiding. Then he decides to hike to Corleone, his
hometown. The camera shifts to various traveling shots,
including his POV climbing the mountains and high-an-
gle shots demonstrating the climb up the hill, creating a
sense of anxiety and fear.

Michael meets Apollonia while trekking through the
fictional city of Corleone.[24] Michael and Apollonia lock
eyes when the women and female children are all together,
probably picking items from the forest or returning from

---

[24] The film was actually shot between Forza D'Agro and Savoca (Pro-
vincia di Messina) because Coppola refused to pay the *pizzo*.

156

the market, as they all have baskets filled with items. The women, Apollonia in particular, appears from behind a row of bushes in bloom with pink flowers resembling oleanders. She is captured amongst these oleanders underscoring her innocence, youth, and passion. According to Edith Box, "In keeping with the Mediterranean origin of the oleander, one legend has it that oleander in Greek mythology means romance and charm."[25] Apollonia's beauty amongst the oleander sparks Michael's interest — he becomes shocked by her beauty, as his Italian bodyguard says, "He was struck like a thunderbolt." In a series of shot-reverse-shots, Michael and Apollonia gaze into each other's eyes and both are clearly attracted to each other.

Following the initial encounter, Michael and his two bodyguards end up drinking and chatting with the bar owner at Bar Vitelli. After various discussions about the beauty of the local women, his bodyguards describe to the bar owner the woman who caught Michael's attention — that woman happens to be Apollonia, the bar owner's daughter. While he first goes to scold her, Michael has one of his bodyguards bring the father out to share his intentions of wooing and marrying her. Through this transactional scene, Old World versus New World mentality is hard to miss. First, the father scolds Apollonia for drawing Michael's interest. Although they obviously never consummated anything, it is Apollonia who takes the brunt of being "slutty." Later, Michael negotiates his future wife, as if an item to be bartered. Essential to understanding this interpretation, we must remember that we are inhabiting

---

[25] Edith Box. "Folklore." International Oleander Society website.

the Old World; Michael never treats Kay this way, as I will later discuss. Thus, Michael and Apollonia's relationship is embraced through the conceptualization that food indeed builds a collateral and Apollonia becomes entwined in this aspect.

When Michael begins the courting process of Apollonia, there is a series of scenes in which food is central. At first, Michael is introduced to all of Apollonia's family, and it seems the entire little town where they live. Michael must continually meet the family. The camera pans in this scene, showing tables full of food, primarily sweets, to be shared at this gathering. The sweets are present to celebrate and welcome Michael into the family. It is a gesture of kindness and illustrates that the family is, in fact, interested in matching Apollonia with Michael. The continuous pans demonstrate how easily Michael blends into both Sicilian life and a life with Apollonia. He eventually becomes one of them.

In the next scene, Michael meets Apollonia's father at what also seems to be Bar Vitelli. A group of people are chatting and drinking. At one point, Michael's POV changes as we understand he is staring at something, but the camera has yet to catch up with his view. Eventually, through a shot-reverse-shot, we, too, engage with the couple, locking of the gaze. Apollonia smiles and grasps the gold necklace around her neck, which Michael gifted her during their first meeting, and they exchange a series of smiles. As they drink and snack, Michael connects with Apollonia across the large table, underscoring again the power food has — consolation and aphrodisiac, as the spectator partakes in their happiness. This scene also brings to life the concept of Old World versus New World. Michael arrives at the bar to converse with Apollonia's father; in fact, the spectator doesn't realize Apollonia's presence until the shot-reverse-shot seconds into the scene. In the Sicilian landscape men clearly dominate the power roles.

In another pre-wedding moment, we note the family chaperoning the date between Michael and Apollonia as they walk through the city, and the family follows, mostly women. In the scene, the camera travels behind the couple with the family. The camera's POV creates the sensation that the spectator partakes in the chaperoning. We note numerous women of a certain age there to both consul and protect Apollonia. While the power remains with the fathers and brothers, the women are present to support and keep an eye on the situation; in the end, Apollonia is one of them and Michael remains an outsider. The folkloric traditions of Sicily surrounded by food and family are set by the gender norms of men. These archaic traditions dominate the landscape in Sicily, even though Michael seeks to empower her.

Once married, the camera assumes a similar function as we join the procession celebrating their wedding. The wedding party arrives in the main square for the wedding reception. Apollonia gifts the guests a *bomboniere* of almonds, another symbol of Sicily. Almonds have been a part of Mediterranean weddings, particularly Italian and Greek, for centuries. Some claim that the Jordan almond is as old as 1350, but more evidence becomes present in the Middle Ages and Renaissance (Johnson). The candies were utilized to celebrate weddings and births. Some research shows that the almonds were encased with honey before the hard candy shell (Johnson). The shape reminds us of an egg and figuratively recalls fertility and rebirth. Often wrapped in a lace pouch, the Italian wedding tradition states that one wraps five almonds together, representing health, wealth, happiness, fertility, and longevity (Johnson). Primarily Apollonia, but even Michael partakes in this Old World tradition celebrating their nuptials. Their wedding feast occurs in the piazza directly in front of Bar Vitelli and again the camera flows through pans and even traveling shots, highlighting the movement predominately of Apollonia. Now that she is married, especially to an American, she too shares in the promise of a better life: health, wealth, happiness, fertility, and longevity.

Yet, these five promises quickly become lies for Apollonia. Although Michael does undertake liberating his new bride, this effort provides fruitless in the end. Apollonia is genuinely in love with Michael and everything he represents. He teaches her not only how to drive but also some basic English. These two skills excite Apollonia. Through teaching Apollonia these talents, one can argue that Michael is preparing her for his return to the U.S., for the New World. But Apollonia never achieves that possibility as she is assassinated in the very "futuristic" machine which represents the New World — Michael's car. In this regard, Apollonia is truly blocked from entry into the New World.

Both before and after his Sicilian experience, Michael is with Kay. Kay proves to be an interesting character throughout the film. First at Connie's wedding, Kay undoubtedly stands out: an orange-shaded dress with a hat. She is the only person wearing a hat and both her and

Michael stand out because of the color of their clothes. Additionally, Michael is the only male family member missing a *bonbonniere* (Mainville). Once seated, Michael strikes up a conversation about Kay's lasagna as both characters stick to themselves as outsiders. Kay begins to ask questions and learns some background information on Don Vito.

Soon before Michael disappears, Michael meets Kay in a hotel room. We are unsure what has happened. All we know is that they had dinner in the hotel room somewhere in New York City. The dinner seems elegant — steak, potatoes, and red wine — and Kay is dressed in a beautiful red dress. She seems concerned about their future. The hotel room has two single beds, both made, but Michael is stuck using one as a dining chair. Although this scene is only suggestive, and creates various possible readings through affect theory, I would like to underline a variance between Kay and Apollonia. In vino veritas, Kay wants answers — she wants to know when she will see Michael again — Michael remains ambiguous and silent, sharing nothing. The focus is on Kay, not Michael. Kay is an aggressor. Maybe it is the food and wine that empowers her, but she knows what she wants and goes after it. She is the New World — she seems to come from a rather established U.S. family with some wealth. Her clothes, hair, speech, and mannerisms all illustrate her social class. When Michael returns to the U.S., who does he court — Kay. Kay is the modern American woman, and this is what Michael longs for, especially when he understands the politic he must establish and preserve. As much as he was in love with Apollonia for her simplicity and beauty, she could

never have made it in the New World. Although Kay represents the New World, Michael, in fact, isn't ready for a
strong, independent woman like Kay. He will always long
to be her equal, as we see, in *Part III*, but he can never
achieve that status. In the end, Michael remains *in-be-
tween,* as Tamburri and Peter Carravetta have theoreti-
cally discussed elsewhere, never fully American but also
always Italian, living half in the Old World, half in the
New World.

PRELIMINARY CONCLUSIONS

Through reconsidering *The Godfather* in this rather
brief contribution, rather than bring the discourse to a
halt, I finish with more questions, more theories, and more
scenes to analyze. While the initial presentation focused
on *The Godfather* series, this space has only allowed for a
concise exploration of *The Godfather*. My intention, however, it to continue this line of discourse analyzing *The
Godfather Part II* and *Part III*. Although the end of this
piece swayed to include an even larger discussion of the
Old World versus the New World, it was interwoven with
the theoretical configuration in which this piece began —
festivals, food, and folklore as a politic of representation.
Food, family, and traditions place a major role in the
power present in society and the influence of the Old/New
World dichotomy plays an active role in understanding
how the politics is conceived.

What seems most compelling of this entire discourse is
that our protagonist, Michael Corleone, is never actually
seen with food in his mouth. While he is regularly surrounded by food, drink, and sweets, Michael does not con-

sume. And yet, food becomes a politic of representation. Food maintains a power structure within the Italian American community, even if Michael never fully partakes. Because he is surrounded by festivals, food, and folklore, he and the family are influenced both directly and indirectly.

WORKS CITED

Bondanella, Peter. 2005. *Hollywood Italians: Dagos, Palookas, Romeos, Wise Guys, and Sopranos*. New York: Continuum.

Brauner, Jesse. 2023. "What's the Meaning of Orange 'Fruit.'" 1 October https://www.symbols.com/symbol/orange-(fruit). Accessed 1 October 2023.

Browne, Nick. 1999. *Francis Ford Coppola's The Godfather Triology*. Cambridge: Cambridge UP.

Campani, Ermelinda M. 2021. "Cibo, dono, patria e famiglia: un approccio etno-antropologico a *The Godfather*." *Imago: studi di cinema e media*, 23:1.

Cavallero, Jonathan J. 2011. *Hollywood's Italian American Filmmakers: Capra, Scorsese, Savoca, Coppola, and Tarantino*. Urbana, Chicago, and Springfield: UIP.

Chatterjee, Arup K. 2021. " 'Luca Brasi Sleeps with the Fishes': The Gastromythology of *The Godfather* Trilogy." in *Food Culture Studies in India: Consumption, Representation and Mediation*, eds. Simi Malhotra et al. Singapore: Springer Nature.

Counihan, Carole M. 1999. *The Anthropology of Food and Body: Gender, Meaning, and Power*. New York: Routledge.

Crumpacker, Bunny. 2006. *The Sex Life of Food*. New York: St. Martin's Press.

De Stefano, George. 2007. *An Offer We Can't Refuse: The Mafia in the Mind of America*. New York: Farrar, Straus and Giroux.

DeSalvo, Louise and Edvige Giunta, eds. 2002. *The Milk of Almonds: Italian American Women Writers on Food and Culture*. New York: The Feminist P.

Girardelli, Davide. 2004. "Commodified Identities: The Myth of Italian Food in the United States." *Journal of Communication Inquiry*. 28:4: 307-324. https://doi.org/10.1177/0196859904267 337. Accessed 1 October 2023.

Johnson, Chapelle. "The History Behind the Jordan Almonds Wedding Tradition." https://www.theknot.com/content/all-about-jordan-almonds. Accessed 1 October 2023.

Keller, James R. 2013. *Food, Film and Culture: A Genre Study*. Jefferson, NC: McFarland.

Larke-Walsh, George S. 2010. *Screening the Mafia: Masculinity, Ehtnicity and Mobsters from The Godfather to The Sopranos*. Jefferson, NC: McFarland.

Lebo, Harlan. 1997. *The Godfather Legacy*. Palmer, AK: Fireside Books.

Lum, Linda. 2022. "The History of Chicken Cacciatore (and Five Recipes)." https://delishably.com/meat-dishes/Exploring-Chicken-Cacciatore. Accessed 1 October 2023.

Mainville, Devin. 2020. "A Great Display of Florals in *The Godfather*." *Floracracy*. https://floracracy.com/blogs/film-tv/a-great-display-of-florals-in-the-godfather. Accessed 1 October 2023.

Messenger, Chris. 2022. *The Godfather and American Culture: How the Corleones Became "Our Gang."* Albany, NY: SUNY P.

MobileAssociate, 2020. "The History of Wedding Cake: Its Origins and Symbolism." *Gala*. June 1. https://www.galafacility.com/the-history-of-wedding-cake-its-origins-and-symbolism/. Accessed 1 October 2023.

Naccarato, Peter. 2017. "There's a mobster in the kitchen: Cooking, eating, and complications of gender in *The Godfather* and *Goodfellas*." In *Representing Italy Through Food*, Peter Naccarato, Zachary Nowak and Elgin K. Eckert, eds. London: Bloomsbury.

Parker, Martin. 2008. "Eating with the Mafia: Belonging and Violence." *Human Relations* 61:7. 989-1006. https://doi.org/10.1177/001872670809 39005. Accessed 1 October 2023.

Rehman, Hafsa. 2018. "Female Identity in Gangster Movies: A Study of *The Godfather* Movie." *Journal of Media Critiques* 13:4 (2018).

Renga, Dana, ed. *Mafia Movies: A Reader*. Toronto: Univ of Toronto Press, 2011.

Santos, Marlisa. 2004. "'Leave the Gun; Take the Cannoli': Food and Family in the Modern American Mafia Film." In *Reel Food: Essays on Food and Film,* Anne L. Bower, ed. New York: Routledge.

Sherlock, Ben. 2023. "*The Godfather*: Why the Oranges Are So Important." *SCREENRANT.* https://screenrant.com/godfather-oranges-important-symbol-why/. Accessed 1 October 2023.

Sutton, David and Peter Wogan. 2003. "The Gun, the Pen, and the Cannoli: Orality and Writing in *The Godfather, Part I.*" *Anthropology and Humanism* 28:2.

Tamburri, Anthony Julian. 2024. "Re-Considering Michael Corleone's Tie: Francis Ford Coppola's *The Godfather"* in *Re-Thinking* The Godfather: *50 Years Later*, edited by Anthony Julian Tamburri. New Fairfield, CT: Casa Lago P.

Tamburri, Anthony Julian. 2021. *Signing Italian/American Cinema: A More Focused Look*. Ambler, PA: Ovunque Siamo P.

Tamburri, Anthony Julian. 2011. "Old World versus New, Or Opposites Attract: Emanuele Crialese's *Nuovomondo"* in *Re-Viewing Italian Americana: Ge-neralities and Specificities on Cinema.* New York: Bordighera P.

Torresi, Ira. 2004. "Identity in a Dish of Pasta: The Role of Food in the Filmic Representation of Italian-Americanness." *Prospero. Rivista di Letteratura Straniere, Comparatistica e Studi Culturali.* 11. https://www.open starts.units.it/handle/10077/ 6275. Accessed 1 October 2023.

Zimmerman, Steve. 2009. "Food in Films: A Star is Born." *Gastronomia* 9:2 (Spring).

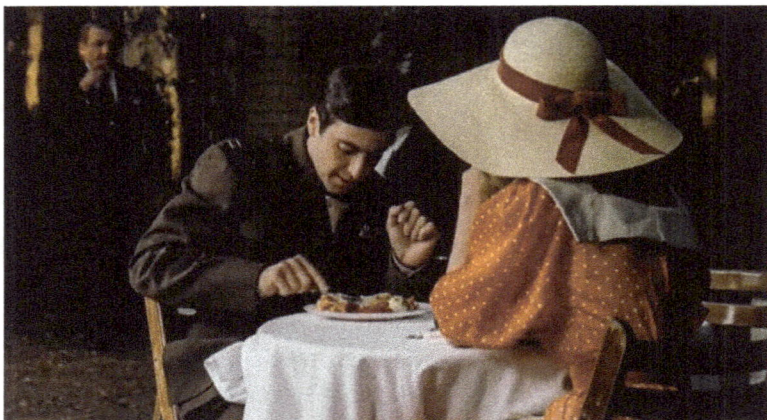

Michael and Kay at Connie's Wedding.

Clemenza shows Michael how to make red sauce for twenty men.

Re-considering Michael Corleone's Tie
Francis Ford Coppola's *The Godfather* and the Rhetoric of Antinomy

ANTHONY JULIAN TAMBURRI

It is surely an understatement to declare that Italian Americans occupy a strong, if often contested, place in American media. One can readily argue that the twentieth-century plight of Italian America began back in 1905, at the onset of the motion picture industry; silent films such as F. A. Dobson's *The Skyscrapers of New York* (1905), Wallace McCutchen's *The Black Hand* (1906), and D. W. Griffith's *The Avenging Conscience* (1914) are early candidates as the springboard for such stereotyping. *Skyscrapers* offered the first appearance of "Dago Pete," a small-time crook who steals his boss's watch while shifting blame onto a co-worker; the second film clearly helped solidify the stereotype of the "black hand"; and the Italian character in this third film is an ill-reputed blackmailer.[1]

Themes such as sex, violence, sentimentality, family relations, and the like would nevertheless dominate a good part of the cinema of and about Italian Americans, generating a contested debate within the Italian/American community at the end of the 20th century about the portrayal of Italians and Italian Americans in United

---

[1] For an acute reading of this early period of United States cinema, see Ilaria Serra's excellent study, especially 102-59, and Giorgio Bertellini's equally insightful study. Also, for those interested in the visual imagery that preceded cinema, I remind the reader of Salvatore LaGumina.

States media overall.[2] Such behavior ultimately figures as a component of the Italian and Italian/American character as cinema developed, within the first half of the 20th century, in the United States, especially with such gangster films as Mervyn Leroy's *Little Caesar* (1930).

From large-scale "godfather" to neighborhood "crook," the mafia theme has indeed left its mark on the American imaginary vis-à-vis the Italian American. For the most part, these celluloid representations and their filmmakers have been hotly debated and, in the majority of cases, vilified. However, some scholars have decided more recently to look at these representations through a different lens: one that interrogates the visual imagery in search of its *prima facie* ironic characteristics and, in so doing, may offer up other readings of the signs therein.[3] That said, I would note that the signifying potentiality of visual images in a film such as *The Godfather* may indeed be greater than the naïve spectator perceives. In this sense, I have in mind (a) the existence of peripheral signs, and (b) its sister concept of "liminal ethnicity," which I have discussed elsewhere.[4]

---

[2] For more on the slash (/) in place of the hyphen (-), see my *To Hyphenate or not to Hyphenate.*

[3] By irony I mean that which sets up a contrast between what seems to be the case and what actually is. In cinema, this contrast between an appearance and a reality would constitute, in the very least, a double layering of meanings, if not polyvalence. Accordingly, then, cinema should have, as Muecke tells us, "both surface and depth, both opacity and transparency, [it] should hold our attention at the formal level while directing it to the level of content." See, D. C. Muecke, *Irony*, 5, as well as Wayne Booth, *The Rhetoric of Irony.*

[4] See my *Italian/American Short Films & Music Videos.*

Peter Bondanella's *Hollywood Italians* (2004) juxta-poses stereotypical roles of Italian Americans in US soci-ety with their portrayals in U.S. cinema, which include primarily immigrants, boxers, Latin lovers, and Mafiosi. He insists that these classifications demonstrate the Ital-ian and Italian/American dedication to admirable values such as the preservation of family and hard work. Much of his book centers on the gangster figure, a representa-tion that may be doing more harm than good for an his-torically informed understanding of the place of Italian Americans in U.S. culture. Bondanella would like to see the Italian American favorably ensconced in American society, despite negative portrayals. Debatable indeed, he points to *The Sopranos* as a prime example of how Italian Americans have moved into mainstream society. Bon-danella also sees in *The Sopranos* a more satisfactory representation of Italian Americans insofar as the char-acters portray a plethora of individuals: mobsters, psy-chotherapists, teachers, lawyers, and of course local, re-gional, and national law enforcement agents.

In demystifying the mafia, one must go beyond the diachronic and thematic and examine potential audience response. George De Stefano's *An Offer We Can't Refuse* (2006) provides a detailed analytical history of represen-tations of mafia in film and television. Regardless of the various successes of the Italian American, he underscores, the "mafia" myth remains the Italian/American icon par excellence. Fred Gardaphe's *From Wiseguys to Wise Men* (2006) examines the mafia in literature and film, ground-ing his readings in the figure of the trickster. Gardaphe demonstrates how such a figure can be (1) held up as a model (as in *The Godfather*), (2) exemplified in a stunted stage, if immature (*Mean Streets*), or (3) ridiculed (as in Giose Rimanelli's novel *Benedetta in Guysterland*). In speaking of the gangster as "artistic device rather than as an actual thug" (xvi), Gardaphe nevertheless recognizes the dilemma raised by the proliferation of the gangster figure. In seeing the gangster as replacing the cowboy, however, he sees this figure as a new "mode of being a man, a roadmap of sorts for masculinity in America[;] a model for moving from poverty or working class to middle or upper class[;]a trope for signifying the gain of cultural power that comes through class mobility" (xvi).

De Stefano and Gardaphe provide the springboard from which to build a semiotic analysis of the evolution and implications of representations of the Italian/American gangster. They offer a one-two punch invitation to a re-examination and a new discussion of this contested figure, one that does not fall back on steadfast determinism (read, outright condemnation) but that allows for a more constructive conversation that could lead to a greater — read, more interpretively flexible — understanding of this truly complex phenomenon that so engulfs Italian Americana.

Of the many things it may signify, *The Godfather* is, first and foremost, the story of an Italian immigrant family's "American" story, its success due to its rise to power albeit within a criminal structure. To some, this is indeed the problem with the film, that it glorifies organized crime and underscores the connection (pardon the pun) of Italian=organized crime (a.k.a. Mafia), as I have already stated here in my "Preface" to this volume.[5] Yet, in looking at the film with a greater interpretive flexibility, as will be apparent herein, we may indeed see the film as more of a condemnation than adulation of the Italian *qua* Mafioso. Through a re-reading of seemingly insignificant signs — Vito Corleone's general dress and Michael's tie — we see that such signs — peripheral and, literally centered, as in Michael's tie — can have much greater semiotic valence than one might initially invest in them.

It is this very sense of semiotic complexity that subtends the visual rhetoric of Coppola's *The Godfather*. From the film's opening scene, the spectator is confronted with a series of signs that are most aptly polysemic. The initial appearance of Don Corleone, for instance, constitutes a clash of possible meanings: Is he the doting father, cuddling a fragile cat, during his daughter's wedding, or the mean-spirited head of a criminal organization? What do we make of Amerigo Bonasera, with that potentially wonderfully hopeful, inspirational name, as it seems only to clash with his profession as undertaker?

There indeed exists a series of seemingly conflicting signs apparent throughout the film. As the movie progresses, the spectator is consistently challenged to decode such signs as possessing one or the other *interpretant*.[6]

---

[5] What the Italian/American community has yet to tackle is how organized crime in Italy vis-à-vis organized crime within the Italian/American community is negotiated and interrogated. Bondanella, De Stefano, and Gardaphe move in this direction, to be sure, but they do not confront this issue head on, as their books have other goals.

[6] I have opted for the Peircean categories of *sign* and *interpretant*, as opposed to the Saussarean couplet of signifier/signified for distin-

Such *coincidentia oppositorum* — the presence of competing imagery and sign functions — is surely part of a rhetorical strategy that is meant to challenge the spectator so that s/he might [re]construct his/her own story that may indeed be the trials and tribulations of a Mafia family, that metaphor for making it in America, as some have wanted to see in the film,[7] or, in fact, something else still.[8] John Paul Russo deconstructs Coppola's *Godfather* series in a keen essay, demonstrating how such a film has succeeded in insinuating itself into the United States collective imaginary. Russo examines the opposition of family and "mafia" in the film, where the latter conquers the former, belying to a certain degree the notion of "mafia" as metaphor for American life.[9]

Whatever the case may be, the figure of the Italian as Mafioso has been a popular one. More than just a crimi-

---

guishing between the image and the concept. For more on the difference, see Floyd Merrell, *Sign, Textuality, World*, especially 3-73.

[7] In this regard, for the most complete study on how Puzo's and Coppola's works have impacted the US collective imaginary, see Christian Messenger, *The Godfather and American Culture*.

[8] Bill Tonelli stated the following: "This radical notion — that even in America, one's own tribe might provide a power structure superior to that of civil authority — is what's really at the heart of The Godfather's appeal. It's why Italian-Americans in particular love the saga, for how it glamorizes and glorifies our values and customs above all others. The Corleones are our Kennedys, except with better morals. // It's also the reason that the rest of America was so taken with it (the book has sold more than 13 million copies thus far): not for its criminality or violence, which is sporadic in any event, but for its vision of an alternative to late-20th-century middle-class mistrust and malaise" (see his "The Godmother."

[9] See his "The Hidden Godfather: Plenitude and Absence in Francis Ford Coppola's *Godfather I* and *II*."

nal, let us not reject the possibility of this figure being, for some, transformed into a counter-cultural icon, one who, while initially part of the downtrodden, can eventually rise to "beat the system," even though the system is a so-called legitimate social structure. This can surely be inferred from Amerigo Bonasera's conversation with Vito Corleone, when Bonasera, in recounting his daughter's ordeal, states, "I went to the police, like a good American" — an act that clearly had no positive result since he was left in the court room "like a fool": the obvious meaning that one needed to work around the system, as, some would say, Vito Corleone did.[10] This seems to have been the case, to some extent, with Puzo's and Coppola's *Godfather*, the prototype for the modern-day gangster. Don Corleone has, in this sense, beaten the system, or so it seems. Coppola, especially, has created a wonderfully rhetorical device that plays well into this primary reading of the film. This is, to be sure, what Marco Greco saw as the "pasta and mobster crap" that Americans associate as Italian characteristics par excellence.[11] In a spirit that complements Gardaphe's, we would not err in stating

---

[10] With regard to Italians in general, let us not ignore that southern Italian fatalism that clearly accompanied the immigrant from Italy to the United States, especially during the first 40 years of Italian emigration. In addition to examples of such skepticism and fatalism that we find in some of the earlier novels — and I would underscore here *Christ in Concrete* (1939) — Carlo Levi's *Christ Stopped at Eboli* (1943) contains a wonderful example of how the so-called legitimate system is seen as one of the many necessary evils humankind must confront, be those evils natural disasters, such as storms, malaria, and other maladies, or institutions such as the Church, Rome, and other social institutions.

[11] See his interview in Parriniello's *Little Italy*.

that films such as *The Godfather* (1972), *Mean Streets* (1973), and/or *GoodFellas* (1989) may indeed provoke a more intense reading that allows the spectator to grasp more firmly their inner semiotic underpinnings. With brief regard to these three films, let us not forget that, in each case, the mob figure was presented as both a physically violent and, often, a sentimentally devoid individual — *in nuce*, a pathetic and despicable human being.

At this juncture, then, I would only remind the reader of certain instances in Coppola's *The Godfather*, scenes that may readily set up a signifying slippery slope of sorts that can easily guide the spectator down a semiotic path that might diverge from an initial reading of Don Corleone as, for example, a self-involved, thuggish Mafioso who killed and had people killed on his way to the top. The first scene that comes to mind is Vito Corleone's meeting with Sollozzo, when he ultimately refuses to engage in the drug-trafficking business. What is significant here is not so much the conversation that takes place as instead the scene's visual aspects. There are seven men in this scene. Six are dressed in dark suits and white shirts and ties, typical for "business" men of this era.[12] Vito Corleone, instead, wears a brownish suit with greenish stripes; his shirt is olive green, and his tie is red-colored based with numerous designs. Thus, contrary to the six other men clearly coiffed in business garb, Don Vito Corleone is dressed like any Italian immigrant grandfather. Whereas no respectable business*man* during this immediate post-World War II era would be seen without a white shirt

---

[12] Clemenza's shirt is the only one with beige stripes.

and dark suit, especially when attending an important meeting as was this one with Sollozzo.[13]

This visual sign of Vito Corleone *qua* the immigrant grandfather is underscored immediately, when he goes to buy fruit, just before being gunned down by Sollozzo's men. Once having dispatched Luca Brasi to get some information from Sollozzo, the scene switches. Subsequently, Vito Corleone, in exiting his office, turns to Fredo and says, "Andiamo, Fredo, tell Paulie to get the car, we're going." Then, once outside, Vito says to his son, "Aspetta, Fred, I'm going to buy some fruit." Both statements involve clear code switching, something readily identified with immigrants, biculturalism, and, according to some, the explicit desire to hold on to one's cultural identity.[14] In addition, the scene is much too reminiscent of immigrant New York for the informed spectator not to take notice. Further still, from the perspective of the camera behind both Vito Corleone and his son, we cast our eyes on a winter street scene of an open vegetable and fruit market, with a burning steel barrel close by, an obvious heat source, quintessential of the era. More than a gangster film, at this juncture, it seems we are viewing an immigrant saga.[15] The question begged here is, of course,

---

[13] See George De Stefano's keenly crafted discussion in his chapter "Don Corleone Was My Grandfather" (95-135). He nicely points out how the Corleones can indeed recall a spectator's Italian family member, as he discusses the hermeneutic relationship between the Italian/American spectator and the film.

[14] See, for example, Carol Myers-Scotton on code-switching.

[15] As an aside, while Vito points out to the *fruttivendolo* what he wants, between the two men once can easily read a poster advertising the January 11, 1946, boxing match between Jake La Motta and

"Would a genuine underworld crime boss, someone like the mythical Don Vito Corleone, be out buying his own fruit and vegetables, and unguarded to boot?"

The other major scene that casts Vito Corleone much more as grandfather than Don is his final scene while playing with his grandson, Anthony, in the proverbial Italian/American vegetable garden.[16] As he engages his grandson in a make-believe game, Vito Corleone feigns being a monster. This scene and all of its signifying capability is one of the more meaningful (pun intended) in the movie vis-à-vis Vito Corleone. Besides the initial fear he instills in Anthony, two important issues stand out: (1) This is the last image we have of Don Corleone, as he runs through the tomato plants, first chasing then being chased by his grandson; (2) As he lie dying, unbeknownst to his grandson, Anthony begins to spray him with what we can only assume to be insect repellent, given the date of the scene, indeed DDT. Such a combination of events is too significant to ignore; it is as if the future generation — the sign of which is /Anthony/ — here now rebuffs that old *monstrous* world of organized crime.[17]

Tommy Bell, which La Motta won in ten rounds. Together with the code-switching, Vito's *italianità* adumbrates here his criminality.

[16] I would remind the reader that this scene is preceded by one in which the Don has clearly passed the baton to Michael. During that meeting, with all men dressed in business attire, Vito Corleone, to the contrary, is wearing a dark shirt, no tie, and a cardigan sweater, already in the role of grandfather in tone and speech, as he assures Clemenza e Tessio.

[17] In retrospect, of course, this scene proves most ironic and truly stands out from the perspective of *Godfather III*, where it becomes clear that Anthony has totally rebuffed the family business and will

Such a reading of Vito Corleone's trajectory compels us to re-consider Michael Corleone's own metamorphosis throughout the film. I am making a distinction here between the 'uninformed' and 'informed' spectator, that individual who is notably experienced in film criticism and may very well unpack *The Godfather* and thus demonstrate the potential in signification that the film offers. Yet, I would go one step further, especially with regard to these "ethnic" films of his, and contend that Coppola's informed, 'Italian/American' spectator may actually have access, to be sure, to a greater inventory of meaning.

I would clarify here that my use of the term "Italian/American spectator" is not grounded in biology. I am not limiting my referents to those who are genetically Italian. I wish to expand my use of the term here as I have done elsewhere.[18] There, I spoke in terms of an *"effective identity* ... in as much as it recognizes the quality of everyday activity in which the individual lives out his/her daily life; an *effective identity* also insofar as it recognizes that what an individual does within a largely Italian milieu unfolds in that way specifically because that person feels his/her actions to be done 'Italian-ly' — *italianamente* we would say in Italian — as part of his/

---

do only as he pleases, sing in the opera, despite his father's previous wishes to the contrary.

[18] See Tamburri (2015). I am converging here with the concept of "Italicity," which Piero Bassetti has been promulgating since 2002. He further elaborated his concept in 2008, and finally in 2015. In specifics, I mentioned Ben Lawton and Rebecca West (2014, 139) and Rebecca West and Jhumpa Lahiri (2017) as examples of those individuals who, not somatically Italian, have acquired an Italian culture equal to if not greater than many who are in fact genetically Italian.

her ordinary existence, and not in any honorary or *affect-ed* sense, but actually 'effective,' such that whatever s/he does — and that s/he knows, as an Italian would — is part of the every-day life of that person. And so, that 'Italian effect' of his/ her daily life is precisely that blending of Italian characteristics and /or *Italianistic-ness* of his/her identity" (Tamburri 2014: 135). It is, I went on to say, "a concept of Italian and/or Italian/American identity, of someone who is not by ethnic origin Italian, but who lives out her/his daily activities, be they professional or personal, if not specifically within, then at least for the most part close to what is coming to be called *Italianità*" (135-36). That said, then, in an attempt to identify some of Scorsese's imagistic acrobatics in light of his informed "Italian/American" spectator's familiarity with certain "Italian" signs, the film indeed affords this second type of informed spectator the privilege of greater signification.

From war hero to "Don Corleone," as Clemenza calls him at the film's closing, there is one seemingly insignificant sign that also undergoes a metamorphosis: it is Michael Corleone's tie. Throughout the film, Michael wears five different ties: red and white; brown; black (at his marriage to Apollonia; at his father's funeral); pinkish-red (when he goes to Las Vegas to "buy out" Moe Greene); and a black, grey, and off-white striped tie. It is indeed this last tie that we first see when, after his return from Italy, he visits Kay at her school. At that moment, Michael is dressed not so much like the busi-ness*man* one might expect, having taken over his father's "business"; rather, he is in quintessential garb we might readily associate with that of the funeral director of the time: derby hat; black overcoat; dark grey pants; and a black, grey, and off-white tie, this last item especially the proverbial calling card of the funeral director's so-called classic "uniform."

Once Michael returns to New York from his Las Vegas hotel-shopping trip, he basically wears only one tie, the black, grey, and off-white one.[19] He wears it, in fact, with a charcoal, striped suit. It is at this juncture in the movie, after the above-mentioned passing of the baton, that Michael's metamorphosis completes itself. Also at this point, we witness the most dramatic example of what I have labeled the film's challenging *coincidentia oppositorum* that subtends *The Godfather*. The famous baptismal scene is a wonderfully efficacious rhetorical montage of both cinematic narrative and the aforementioned structuring of opposites.

The alternation of scenes from the highly ornate church setting of the sacrament of baptism to the individual murders ordered by Michael underscores in this episode the film's semiotic antinomy: the movie's most significant juxtaposition of scenes. It pits the highest of Catholic celebrations — the cleansing of original sin — with the most despicable of human acts — murder. Having now acquired his role of godfather to his nephew, Michael must, at this time, complete his own cleansing of his newly inherited "business" through Carlo Rizzi's murder. That accomplished, Michael himself has forthwith been truly baptized as "heir to his father, heir to

---

[19] The only divergence is at his father's funeral, where he wears a solid black tie.

his sin,"[20] thus becoming, in the most clichéd manner possible, a "godfather" twice over.

Such antinomical structuring is present in the scene after Michael's return from his Las Vegas trip. In the family compound garden, talking with his father about the "business," numerous things stand out in this regard. First, while Vito Corleone is dressed as *everyman*'s grandfather, Michael, in business garb, is wearing his black, grey, and off-white tie. Second, as Vito Corleone offers him advice about the business and his safety, as well, their conversation is peppered with questions and facts about the family, Michael's children especially, which distracts the spectator's attention from one subject (cold-blooded business) and shifts it to another (general welfare of family members). Third, at one point, Vito is a *forgetful grandfather*, repeating himself, to some degree, while his son now adamantly reminds his father that he will "handle it, [he] told [his father he] can handle it..." This is followed by a fourteen-second silence, as Vito gets to his feet and eventually goes into his famous speech about how he did not want this for Michael; he wanted Michael to be the one "to hold the strings, senator Corleone, Governor Corleone, something..." With the spectator distracted by this doting father's unfulfilled wishes for his youngest son's future, the conversation ends with Vito slipping back into his godfather role, firmly reminding his son that "whoever comes to [him] with this Barzini meeting, he's the traitor. Don't forget that!"

---

[20] See James Thomas Chiampi's insightful semiotic reading, "Resurrecting *The Godfather*."

The spectator, at this point is brought back to the reality of the film's basic premise, the brutal life of organized crime.[21]

Vito's apparent grandfatherly dress and behavior is a counterpoint to his Don Vito *persona*, for sure. Similarly, Michael's metamorphosis, signaled by what seems to be his favorite tie, is a counterpoint to his initial war-hero status. These two antinomical examples can only underscore the possibility of an interpretive strategy on the informed spectator's part and/or a rhetorical device on Coppola's part, even if we cannot divine authorial intentionality.[22] Such a reading is underscored by what we may now identify as a logical bracketing. First, let us not forget that Michael Corleone is dressed in the same suit, shirt, and tie during the last twenty-seven minutes of the film. Second, this is the moment he defines his strategy for the takeover and, eventually, completes the task. Third, the film closes with Michael Corleone, in its penultimate scene, literally framed within the door-jamb, surrounded by Clemenza and two others, with

---

[21] Two scenes separate this father-son conversation and the above-described baptism scene: one is Vito's death while playing with his grandson; the other is Vito's funeral. These two scenes overall, I would submit, underscore the film's *coincidentia oppositorum*, as they, too, though ever so briefly, distract the spectator from the film's basic storyline of organized crime, until Tessio makes his move at the end of Vito's funeral scene.

[22] Umberto Eco deals nicely with this in "*Intentio Lectoris.*" Indeed, in the spirit of semiotic flexibility, we might also consider how Vito's dress and connections to family, garden, traditions, etc. might also situate him more as representing "old mafia" (read, the old world with its coincidental value system) that ultimately conflicts with the new world, with the way Michael positions himself.

Clemenza, as mentioned above, uttering the final two words of the film, "Don Corleone," both a greeting and, dare we say, announcement of Michael's ultimate success. He is, at this point, both godfather and — dressed, as he is — undertaker, having now buried, so to speak, his five enemy "caporegimes."

In closing, then, there remains one more sign to invest with meaning. At a little more than mid-way through the movie, Don Corleone must now call upon Bonasera for that favor he thought he might never have to ask. When he arrives at Bonasera's funeral parlor with his son's cadaver, we see Amerigo dressed in full garb, wearing, at center screen, his funeral director's tie — a black, grey, and off-white striped design similar to what Michael dons for the first time during his visit to Kay. It is also the same tie Michael will wear during the last twenty-seven minutes of the film, when he ultimately solidifies his position as heir to Don Vito Corleone. Thus, we think back to the beginning of the movie, which opens with Amerigo Bonasera, a true undertaker, whose conversation with Don Corleone first signals meaning and logic, as Don Corleone reminds him that the murder of his daughter's violent would-be rapists would not be "justice," since justice signifies otherwise — a one for one, which this would not be. That said, the film's opening conversation signals to the spectator that there are indeed various modes in which signs may be manipulated throughout, which then may readily become part of the spectator's responsibility in investing meaning into signs. Now, at the end of the movie, as we the spectators have witnessed various semiotic machinations along the way, we end our viewing with the final confirmation of Michael Corleone, godfather par excellence, dressed in his undertaker garb. The closing of the door in Kay's face — literally, the final scene — is only an addendum to Michael's framed portrait, as it reminds us spectators that Michael's lie to Kay is only symptomatic of his manipulation of sign functions (read, meaning; read, truth), as Bonasera had tried to do with Don Vito Corleone at the film's opening.

Given the notably problematic narrative structure of *The Godfather*, as the six contributors to this volume have already demonstrated,[23] we might consider borrowing from and paraphrasing Jean-François Lyotard as an appropriate way to close, for now. For if the film a director "produces [is] not in principle governed by pre-established rules [i.e., canon formation], and [it] cannot be judged according to a determining judgment, by applying familiar categories to [said film]" (81), then one may very well be able to look elsewhere for interpretive strategies. Precisely because, as Lyotard continues, "[t)hose rules and categories are what the work ... is looking for." We might then say that the filmmaker, as in Coppola's case, is "working [not necessarily] without rules" but is adding to the already formulated set of rules and hence adds to the overall narrative reservoir established in part by the so-called "familiar categories" of a "determining judgment." That said, the informed Italian/American spectator, precisely because of his/her particular cultural reservoir, may very

---

[23] Others still have underscored Coppola's dexterous, narratological antinomy. See any of the following: Browne, Cavallero, D'Acierno, Ferraro, Thomas J., Lawton, Phillips.

well be able to establish, as s/he proceeds, particular interpretive strategies "of what will have been [seen]." This special spectator, then, will proceed to recodify and reinterpret the seemingly arbitrary — that is, non-canonical — signs.

Such an interpretive act relies on the individual's time and place, and in the case of *The Godfather*; the time is the 1960s and 1970s, and the place is the semiosphere of the Italians from Little Italy. These, among other things, very well constitute the particular intertextual reservoir of the informed Italian/American spectator for which, in our case, a tie is sometimes more than a tie.[24]

WORKS CITED

Bassetti, Piero. 215. *Svegliamoci italici: manifesto per un future glocal*. Venice: Marsilio.

Bassetti, Piero. 2008. *Italici. Il possibile futuro di una community globale*. Milan: Casagrande.

Bassetti, Piero. 2002. *Challenge of a Global Age*, Paulo Ianni and George F. McLean, eds.; Washington, DC: The Council for Research in Values and Philosophy. 13-24.

Bertellini, Giorgio. 2010. *Italy in Early American Cinema: Race, Landscape, and the Picturesque*. Bloomington: Indiana UP.

Bondanella, Peter. 2004. *Hollywood Italians: Dagos, Palookas, Romeos, Wise Guys, and* Sopranos. New York: Continuum.

Booth, Wayne. 1961. *The Rhetoric of Irony*. Chicago: U Chicago P.

---

[24] This essay first appeared as ""Michael Corleone's Tie: Francis Ford Coppola's *The Godfather*" (2011); it appears here in a significantly modified and expanded version. It also borrows from my essay (Tamburri 2017) on Martin Scorsese's *Mean Streets* and the notion of code-switching and of the related comparison between the "uninformed" versus the "informed Italian/American spectator."

Browne, Nick. 1999. *Francis Ford Coppola's* Godfather *Trilogy*. Cambridge, UK: Cambridge UP.

Cavallero, Jonathan J. 1999. "Gangsters, Fessos, Tricksters, and Sopranos: the Historical Roots of Italian American Stereotype Anxiety," *Journal of Popular Film and Television* (Summer): 50-63.

Chiampi, James Thomas. 1978. "Resurrecting *The Godfather*," *MELUS* 5.4 (Winter): 18-31.

D'Acierno, Pellegrino. 1999. *"Cinema Paradiso*: The Italian American Presence in American Cinema." *The Italian American Heritage*. New York: Garland. 563-690.

De Stefano, George. 2006. *An Offer We Can't Refuse: The Mafia in the Mind of America*. New York: Faber and Faber.

Eco, Umberto. 1988. "*Intentio Lectoris*: The State of the Art," *Differentia, review of italian thought*. 2 (Spring): 147-68.

Ferraro, Thomas J. 1993. "Blood in the Marketplace: The Business of Family in *The Godfather* Narratives," *Ethnic Passages: Literary Immigrants in Twentieth-Century America*. Chicago: U Chicago P.

Gardaphe, Fred. 2006. *From Wiseguys to Wise Men: The Gangster and Italian American Masculinities*. New York, Routledge.

LaGumina, Salvatore. 1973. *WOP: A Documentary History of Anti-Italian Discrimination*. San Francisco: Straight Arrow Books.

Lawton, Ben. 2002. "Mafia and the Movies: Why Is Italian American Synonymous with Organized Crime?" Anna Camaiti Hostert, and Anthony Julian Tamburri, Eds. *Screening Ethnicity*. Boca Raton: Bordighera P. 69-95.

Levi, Carlo. 2006. *Christ Stopped at Eboli*. Trans. F. Frenaye; intro. Mark Rotella. New York: Farrar, Straus and Giroux.

Merrell, Floyd. 1992. *Sign, Textuality, World*. Bloomington: Indiana UP.

Myers-Scotton, Carol. 1993. *Social Motivations for Codeswitching: Evidence from Africa*. Oxford: Clarendon.

Messenger, Christian. 2001. *The Godfather and American Culture: How the Corleones Became Our Gang*. Albany, NY: SUNY P.

Muecke, D. C. 1970. *Irony*. London: Methuen.

Little Italy. Dir. Will Parriniello. 1995.

Phillips, Gene D. 2004. *Godfather: The Intimate Francis Ford Coppola*. Lexington: UP of Kentucky.

Russo, John Paul. 1986. "The Hidden Godfather: Plenitude and Absence in Francis Ford Coppola's *Godfather I* and *II*" in *Support and Struggle: Italians and Italian Americans in a Comparative Perspective*. Ed. Joseph L. Tropea *et al*. Staten Island, NY: AIHA. 255–81

Serra, Ilaria. 1997. *Immagini di un Immaginario: L"emigrazione Italiana negli Stati Uniti fra I Due Secoli (1890-1924)*. Verona, Italy: CIERRE, 1997

Tamburri, Anthony Julian. 2017. "Il sistema di segni del cinema italiano/americano: *code-switching* e la significabilità di *Mean Streets* di Martin Scorsese," *Ácoma* (Fall-Winter): 108-121.

Tamburri, Anthony Julian. 2015. "The "Italian" Writer: Reflections on a New Category" in *Transcending Borders, Bridging Gaps: Italian Americana, Diasporic Studies, and the University Curriculum*. Anthony Julian Tamburri and Fred Gardaphé, eds. New York: Calandra Institute. 135-42.

Tamburri, Anthony Julian. 2014. *Re-reading Italian Americana: Generalities and Specificities on Literature and Criticism*. Madison, NJ: Fairleigh Dickinson UP.

Tamburri, Anthony Julian. 2011a. "Michael Corleone's Tie: Francis Ford Coppola's *The Godfather*" in *Mafia Movies. A Reader*. Dana Renga, ed. Toronto: U Toronto P. 94-101. Slightly modified as "Michael Corleone's Tie: Francis Ford Coppola's *The Godfather* and the Rhetoric of Antinomy" (2011). 94-101.

Tamburri, Anthony Julian. 2011b. *Re-viewing Italian Americana: Generalities and Specificities on Cinema*. New York: Bordighera P. 80-91.

Tamburri, Anthony Julian. 2002. *Italian/American Short Films & Music Videos: A Semiotic Reading*. West Lafayette: Purdue UP.

Tamburri, Anthony Julian. 1991. *To Hyphenate or not to Hyphenate: the Italian/American Writer: Or, An* Other *American?* Montréal: Guernica.
Tonelli, Bill. 2003. "The Godmother: The Woman Who Taught Mario Puzo the Value of Secrecy," *Slate.com* (May).

Michael after the baptism and just before he receives Connie.

Bonasera looks down at Sonny's mutilated body.

Michael at Connie's baby's baptism.

CONTRIBUTORS

REBECCA BAUMAN is Associate Professor of Italian in the Department of Modern Languages and Cultures at Fashion Institute of Technology, SUNY, where she is also affiliate faculty in the Department of Film, Media and Performing Arts. She teaches courses on Italian language, Italian American cultural studies, Italian fashion culture, and film studies, and has published numerous articles and book chapters in such publications as the *Journal of Italian Cinema and Media Studies, Italian Studies,* and *Film, Fashion & Consumption.* She is Film and Digital Media reviews editor for the journal *Italian American Review,* and she is a frequent lecturer on fashion studies and contemporary and classical Italian film. In 2023, she was awarded an NEH Landmarks of American History and Culture grant for her project entitled "Creative Spaces/Contested Spaces: Reinterpreting Italian American Public Art in New York City." She is currently working on a monograph on the role of fashion in Italian and Italian American representations of organized crime.

RYAN CALABRETTA-SAJDER is Associate Professor and Section Head of Italian and Associate Director of Gender Studies at the University of Arkansas, Fayetteville, where he teaches courses in Italian, African and African American Studies, Comparative Literature and Cultural Studies, Film and Media, Jewish, and Gender Studies. He is the author of *Divergenze in celluloide: colore, migrazione e identità sessuale nei film gay di Ferzan Özpetek* (*Celluloid Divergences: Color, Migration, and Sexual Identity in the Gay Series of Ferzan Özpetek*) with Mimesis editore, editor of *Pasolini's Lasting Impressions: Death, Eros, and Literary Enterprise in the Opus of Pier Paolo Pasolini* with Fairleigh Dickinson University Press, and co-editor of *Theorizing the Italian Diaspora: Selected Essays* with IASA, and *Italian Americans On*

189

Screen: Challenging the Past, Re-Theorizing the Future with Lexington Books. He is also the founding and current editor of *Diasporic Italy: Journal of the Italian American Studies Association.*

DONNA CHIRICO is Professor of Psychology and former Dean for the School of Arts and Sciences at York College of The City University of New York (CUNY) who has spent She has spent 25+ years teaching and working with underserved, urban college students. Additionally, she has an appointment as Resident Faculty at the John D. Calandra Italian American Institute. Her academic career began with field research in India studying moral and spiritual development, which constitutes the foundation of her current research program. The objective of this work is to understand the function of esoteric or transcendent imagination in personal development, attainment of valued goals, and psychological well-being. Related to this, matters of personal identity formation are explored to understand how ethnic identity contributes to the psychological development of the self, specifically in Americans of Italian heritage and more broadly within the Italian Diaspora. As part of the Italian Diaspora Studies Summer Seminar, she teaches the unit, "Identity in the Italian Diaspora: Psychological Perspectives." She serves on the editorial boards of the journals, *The Italian American Review* and *Diasporic Italy*; and, given numerous presentations and published in the area of Italian American and Italian Diaspora Studies.

GEORGE DE STEFANO is a New York-based writer and editor specializing in culture, politics, and social issues. He is the author of *An Offer We Can't Refuse: The Mafia in the Mind of America* (Farrar, Straus, Giroux) and a contributor to numerous other books, including *The Routledge History of Italian Americans,*

Our Naked Lives: Essays from Gay Italian American Men (Bordighera Press), *Mafia Movies* (University of Toronto), *The Essential Sopranos Reader* (University of Kentucky Presses), and *Reggae, Rasta, and Revolution* (Schirmer). He is working on a book about the Sicilians of New Orleans. His articles, essays, and reviews have appeared in *The Nation, Newsday, Film Comment, The Advocate, The Italian American Review, Gay and Lesbian Review Worldwide,* and the online publications *PopMatters, Rootsworld,* the *New York Journal of Books, La Voce di New York,* and I-Italy.

FRED GARDAPHE is Distinguished Professor of English and Italian/American Studies at Queens College/CUNY and the John D. Calandra Italian American Institute. Gardaphe is Associate Editor of *Fra Noi,* editor of the Series in Italian American Studies at State University of New York Press, and co-founding co-editor of *Voices in Italian Americana, a literary journal and cultural review.* He is past-President of the American Italian Historical Association (1996-2000) now the Italian American Studies Association, past-President of MELUS: The Society for the Study of Multi-Ethnic Literature of the United States, and the Working Class Studies Association. His books include *Italian Signs, American Streets: The Evolution of Italian American Narrative, Dagoes Read: Tradition and the Italian/American Writer, Moustache Pete is Dead!, Leaving Little Italy,* and *From Wiseguys to Wise Men: Masculinities and the Italian American Gangster.* His latest study, *Funny How?: Humor and Irony in Italian American Culture* is forthcoming with Penn State University Press

CHIARA MAZZUCCHELLI is Associate Professor and Dr. Neil Euliano Chair in Italian Studies at the University of Central Florida. She directs the Italian program and teaches courses on Italian language and culture as well as seminars on Italian and Italian-

American literature. From Spring 2017 to Fall 2021, she served as the Associate Chair of the Department of Modern Languages and Literatures, and during the academic year 2019-2020, she held the position of Provost Faculty Fellow. She is the author of *The Heart and the Island: A Critical Study of Sicilian American Literature*, published by SUNY Press in 2015, and has contributed articles to journals such as *Italica, Nuova Prosa, Forum Italicum, Journal of Modern Italian Studies, Altreitalie*, and *Italian Americana*. From 2009 to 2018, she was Editor-in-Chief of the semi-annual peer-reviewed journal *Voices in Italian Americana (VIA)*.

ANTHONY JULIAN TAMBURRI is Dean of the John D. Calandra Italian American Institute (Queens College, CUNY) and Distinguished Professor of European Languages and Literatures. He is co-founder and co-director of Bordighera Press, past president of the Italian American Studies Association and of the American Association of Teachers of Italian. Concentrating on cinema, literature, and semiotics, he has authored 20 books in both English and Italian, and more than 130 peer-reviewed essays and book chapters. Three of his most recent books include: *The Columbus Affair: Imperatives for an Italian/American Agenda* (2021); *Signing Italian/American Cinema: A More Focused Look* (2021); and *A Politics of [Self-]Omission: The Italian/American Challenge in A Post-George Floyd Age* (2022). He is executive producer and host of Calandra's TV program, *Italics,* produced in collaboration with CUNY TV. In 2010, the title of *Cavaliere dell'Ordine al Merito della Repubblica Italiana* was conferred upon him *motu proprio* by the Hon. Giorgio Napolitano, then President of Italy.

INDEX

NOTE TO READER: Throughout the index, *Godfather I* refers to *The Godfather* (Puzo and Coppola, 1972), *Godfather II* refers to *The Godfather Part II* (Coppola, 1974) and *Godfather III* refers to *The Godfather Part III* (Coppola, 1990). *The Godfather* series includes both Puzo's writings and Coppola's films.

relationship with Conne, 139, 156

relationship with Michael, 136–37, 179

Carmela Corleone (Mamma), 98, 110–11, 155–56

Castellano, Paul, 87–88

Cay Johnston, David, 87–88

Cazale, John, 111n1, 119

Chatterjee, Arup K., 125–26

Christ in Concrete (Donato), 53, 55–56, 64, 173n10

Christ Stopped at Eboli (Levi), 173n10

Clemenza
food symbolism associated with, 138, 148–52
relationship with Michael, 151, 178, 182
understanding of Mafia violence, 25, 105, 147–48

clothing, symbolism of, 37–38, 130, 152, 160–61, 171, 174–75, 176n15, 178–83, 179n19

code-switching, ix, 154, 175, 176

Cohen, Joshua, 73

Cohn, Roy, 75

community, Italian American, 3, 34, 50, 127, 149, 135, 171n5

compareggio (godparenthood), 50–51

Connie Corleone Rizzi
at chicken cacciatore dinner, 156
as childlike, 6
evolution of, 128–29, 129n7, 139
wedding celebration, 24, 97–99, 129–32, 138–39

Connor Roy (in *Succession*), 117

The Conversation, "Who's who in the *Godfather* version of

Trump's White House," 72–73

Coppola, Francis Ford
camera angles during assassination scenes, 132–33
complex narrative approach, 183–84, 183n23
depiction of Little Italy, 33–34
on *The Godfather* as allegory about capitalism, 35, 67, 88–89
portrayal of early 20th century Sicily, 28
sympathies for Fredo, 112
on use of oranges in films, 142–43

Corleone, Sicily, Mafia associations, 39, 143

Counihan, Carole M., 127, 134

Crumpacker, Bunny, 127

Culkin, Kieran, 118

Cuomo, Chris, 19, 72, 115

Cuomo, Mario, 18

D'Agostino, Guido, 63–64

Dal Cerro, William, 22n2, 57

The Dark Arena (Puzo), 52

Deanna Corleone, 105–6

death, association of oranges with, 142–43

De Bonis, Antonio, 86–87

Denaro, Matteo Messina, 70, 83n1

De Niro, Robert, 22n3, 95–96

DeRosa, Tina, 57

DeSalvo, Louise, 125, 127

De Stefano, George, 3, 169–70, 171n5, 175n13

di Donato, Pietro, 52, 53, 55, 56, 64

Di Marco, Luigi Arcuri, 32

Di Prima, Diana, 57

Dobson, F. A., 167

196

Italian American response
to, 53–54
negative criticism as a work
of art, 57–60
political relevance, 67–68
writing of, 52–53
godparent role, 50–51
Gotti, John, 73–74
Graham, Lindsay, 76–77
Gramsci, Antonio, 67
Greco, Marco, 173
Griffith, D. W., 167

Harwicke, Catherine, 22n3
Hollywood Italians (Bondanella), 169
homosociality, 9–10, 12–13.
See also masculine identity
honor
and the Cosa Nostra, 89–90
"Don" title as, 26
godparent role, 51
Michael's war heroism, 36,
130, 130n9
Vito Corleone's sense of, 36
"How The Godfather Explains
GOP Leadership Politics"
(Pitney Jr.), 77
How the Other Half Lives (Riis), 33
Hulsman, John C., 78–79
Hyman Roth, 104

identity development. *See also*
Italian Americans
assimilation process, 63, 172
as continuous, ongoing, 11–12
ethnic roles, 1–2, 6
impact of gangster movies
on, 21–22, 56–58
relationships and group affiliations, 2, 7–8, 12
I fasci siciliani (Renda), 29

I Malavoglia (Verga), 28
informed vs. uninformed spectators, 124, 124n3
irony, cinematic, 114, 132, 152,
153, 155, 168, 168n3, 176n17
Italian Americans. *See also*
family, food and wine; masculine identity
assimilation struggles, ii,
33–34, 40, 67
as culture hero, 63
discrimination against, vii
early media portrayals,
167–68
identity issues, 96
the immigrant grandfather,
175–76, 175n13
impact of *The Godfather*, 4,
22–23, 55–60, 171–72
informed understandings,
124, 144, 144n19, 175,
177–78, 181, 183–84
Italian effective identity,
177–78, 177n18
levels of relationship, 50
Michael's in-betweenness,
162–63
stereotyped representations, vii, 2–3, 8–9, 18–19,
21, 43–44, 167, 169, 170
validity of studying experience of, 42–43, 42n9
Italian Signs (Gardaphe), 36
"Italicity," 177n18
Italy
Great Emigration, 32n6
male-only boar hunts, 9–10
southern, fatalism in, 173n10
unification of, impacts in
Sicily, 30–31
"From Italy to America"
course, 23, 42, 42n9

Jack Woltz, Hagen's meeting with, 142
Johnny Fontane, at Connie's wedding, 138
Johnson, Boris, 68

Kay Adams-Corleone
  disregard for, 6
  introductory scene, 98, 130–32
  relationship with Michael, 99, 150, 158, 162, 182–83
  as unique, 160–62
Keller, J. R., 126–27
Kendall Roy (in *Succession*), 117–18
Kushner, Jared, 73

La Cosa Nostra (Sicilian Mafia). *See also* the Mafia
  populist claims, 83n1, 89
  privatized services, 70
  pursuit of self-interest, 69, 80
  structure, 86–87
La Motta, Jake, 175–76n15
Lawton, Ben, 21–22, 177n18
Leave the Gun, Take the Cannoli (Seal), vii–ix
Leigh, Danny, 68
Leonetti, Philip, 88
Leroy, Mervyn, 168
Levi, Carlo, 173n10
"Liberty" (Verga), 28
"A Literature Considering Itself: The Allegory of Italian America" (Viscusi), 64
Little Caesar (Leroy), 168
Little Italy, New York, 33–34
Logan Roy (*Succession*), 117
Luca Brasi
  bulletproof vest-wrapped fish, 24

at Connie's wedding, 131–32
  death scene, 146–47
"Luna Mezzo Mare" (song), 24, 138
Lupo, Salvatore, 84–85
Lyotard, Jean-François, 183

Machiavelli, Niccolò, 67
the Mafia
  concerns about showcasing in The Godfather, vii
  decline in the US, 89
  extortion by, 82, 156n24
  as family, Nuichael's dedication to, 145
  Gardaphe's explorations, 48–49
  hostility to leftist politics, 70
  legitimate businesses and, 86
  mafiosa / mafiosi, 83, 83n1
  media representations, 1, 82, 169–70
  as metaphor for American life, 172
  parallels with corporate capitalism, 79–80
  in Sicily, 38–39, 82–84
  student fascination with, 19–20
  transactional relationships, 74, 84
  as a world of its own, 80–81
Mafia Business: The Mafia Ethic and the Spirit of Capitalism (Arlacchi), 83–85
Mafia Mamma (Harwicke, film), 22n3
Mangione, Jerre, 52
Mark McCluskey, assassination of, 153–55
masculine identity
  buddy movies, 8–9

DIASPORA

As *diaspora* is the dispersion or spread of people from their original homeland, this series takes its name in the intellectual spirit of willful dispersion of subject matter and thought. It is dedicated to publishing those studies that in various and sundry ways either speak to or offer new methods of analysis of the Italian diaspora.

Carmelo Fucarino. *Two Italian Geniuses in New York: Broken American Dreams*. ISBN 978-1-955995-05-4. 2023.

CASA LAGO PRESS EDITORIAL GROUP

www.ingramcontent.com/pod-product-compliance
Lightning Source LLC
Chambersburg PA
CBHW061732270326
41928CB00011B/2199